ORIGINS OF CONSCIOUSNESS

ORIGINS OF CONSCIOUSNESS

*HOW THE SEARCH TO UNDERSTAND THE NATURE
OF CONSCIOUSNESS IS LEADING TO
A NEW VIEW OF REALITY*

ADRIAN DAVID NELSON

METARISING BOOKS
2015

Copyright © 2015 by Adrian David Nelson

All rights reserved. This book or any portion thereof may not be reproduced or used in any manner whatsoever without the express written permission of the publisher except for the use of brief quotations.

First Printing: 2015

ISBN 978-1-329-29877-4

Metarising books
3 Wellington Road,
Nottingham,
England
NG14 5GQ

www.originsofconsciousness.com

Contact: adrian.david.nelson@gmail.com

Cover photograph by Derek Kind

For my father

CONTENTS

1. THE QUESTION OF CONSCIOUSNESS — 2
2. THE INNER LANDSCAPE — 23
3. MIND AND MATTER — 43
4. ANOMALOUS OBSERVATIONS — 58
5. CONSCIOUSNESS AS AN ORDERING PRINCIPLE — 69
6. ENTANGLED PERCEPTIONS — 94
7. SHARING INNER SPACE — 99
8. MIND IN TIME — 110
9. THE VIEW FROM HERE — 122
10. THE MEANINGFUL UNIVERSE — 131
11. HORIZONS — 166

   REFERENCES — 190

'In the history of the collective as in the history of the individual, everything depends on the development of consciousness.'

Carl Gustav Jung

1. THE QUESTION OF CONSCIOUSNESS

Consciousness is that inner awareness each of us has. It is the witness to our thoughts, and ultimately, who we really are. In this book, the term 'consciousness' will be used to describe any form of awareness, regardless of complexity or degree. But what *is* consciousness? Are thoughts things? How does the felt world of experience arise from the soft, wet tissue of our brains? Are we no more than our brains? And if so, what is it about brains that permit this experiencing center in the physical universe? Consciousness is the vehicle of all value and meaning. It is the ontological fountainhead, not just of the means to attribute significance, but of significance itself. Without it, there could be no meaning or value in the universe. It is then, in a certain sense, all that really matters. Such centrality sits uneasily with our competing suspicions of the insignificance of life in the cosmos. Despite our intimacy with consciousness, it seems no less astonishing that within us the universe has evolved a means through which it experiences itself. The existence of this inner dimension is so imminent to us, and yet it is perhaps the deepest mystery we face. Is consciousness an atomized illusion of biological organisms in a meaningless universe, or is it an extension of nature's ongoing creative process? Are we mere spectators of reality, or are we active *participators*? There has never and will never be a question deeper or more consequential than the question of consciousness. Beyond our personal beliefs, how we collectively respond to this question has far reaching implications to our civilization in the values it holds, and the choices it makes. Our answers are the basis of our religious and spiritual beliefs, the structure of the institutions we build around us, and the values we pass to our children. It deeply informs our relationships to each other, the environment, and other species. We will explore how the question of consciousness has continued to resist all attempts at explanation through the standard reductive materialism that has characterized science of the last three hundred years, and how this has led a growing number of respected scientists and philosophers to argue that an expansion of science will be necessary to understand it. We will explore how a trend in thinking is moving toward deeper views of mind, to regard consciousness or awareness as an intrinsic rather than incidental feature of the natural world. I will refer to this modest, though growing shift in secular thinking as the *intrinsic consciousness movement*. It is a movement leading both to a radical new understanding of the mind and a profound new understanding of reality.

◆ ◆ ◆

The great strides of modern science have provided deep insight into the structure and tendencies of nature, engendered planet-transforming technologies, lifesaving medicine and unprecedented access to information. Yet, for all its successes in improving human life, science has failed to provide any resounding consensus on the very thing that conceived it – the conscious mind. We know directly that we are conscious, and we intuit that other people are too, but even acclaimed authorities on the subject disagree about whether dogs have it – and if they do, why a fish does or does not. Nor have they been able to agree on the necessary and sufficient conditions that accompany it. The problem rises from the fact that we simply cannot tell by examining a brain why it should be conscious. A popular approach of past decades has been to describe mental states in terms of their functions, imagining the mind like software running on the hardware of the brain.[1] But this approach, known as 'functionalism', is now widely recognized to be insufficient to explain consciousness. If mental states are functions, why exactly does conscious experience lawfully accompany them?

Between the inputs from the environment and the outputs of behavior, there's something more, an *experience* of being in those states. Why, as philosopher Thomas Nagel asks, is there 'something it is like' to be us?[2] This is often referred to as the 'hard problem' of consciousness, a term brought into popular thinking by the philosopher David Chalmers.[3] It is conceivable, Chalmers points out, that an advanced enough understanding of the brain will capture the full range of its physical, behavioral and functional operations, illuminating all of the yet to be understood processes of cognition. However, he argues, even with this full physical account of the brain, the hard problem of consciousness will still remain – a mysteriously inexplicable first-person account of our small part of the universe. All around us we observe new phenomena arising from complex systems, but of all the highly complex phenomena of the world, from weather to ecosystems, it is at least conceivable that a full account of the interacting parts involved will predict even the most complex emergent behaviors. Consciousness, on the other hand, is different. There doesn't seem to be any reason why several billion interacting neurons should lawfully give rise to subjective experience. All other emergent phenomena in the world can be understood in terms of their behavior, yet consciousness characterizes a distinctly inner subjective perspective. How can we meaningfully transition from talking about physical processes to mental experiences? Even the faintest glimmer of awareness seems categorically different to no experience at all. The enduring question of how mental states could emerge from physical processes is the hard problem of consciousness. It is a problem that seems more than just very difficult; from the perspective of our standard materialism, it's not clear what a solution would even look like.

In the early 20th century, psychology was in the midst of an identity crisis. Its scientific status had been challenged by the difficulty of performing rigorous study of the inner psychological states of the conscious mind. The resulting approach, known as *behaviorism*, set the contents of consciousness aside in favor of the exclusive study of external behaviour.[4] As the field advanced, however, it became increasingly clear that denying mental states left out the true essence of psychology. Sensations, emotions, feelings and desires – these were what made us who we are as individuals. While in some relative obscurity, the problem of the mind's relationship to the brain and body continued to be discussed by philosophers. It wasn't until the 1980s however, that consciousness re-entered the mainstream scientific lexicon. Francis Crick, the celebrated biologist and co-discoverer of the structure of DNA, and his new colleague, Caltech trained neuroscientist Christof Koch, announced a new scientific program dedicated to capturing the neurobiological correlates of consciousness. Riding high on his recent breakthrough with DNA, Crick now had hopes of unlocking that other great mystery of life: human sentience. Through their study, and the research it inspired, many new discoveries about cognition were achieved, and yet precisely how specific cognitive processes gave rise to subjectivity remained a seemingly intractable enigma.[5] There didn't seem to be any middle ground between the objective physical facts true of the brain, and the subjective world of consciousness. Any explanation seems ultimately forced to take no less than a leap of pure faith from the objectively physical to the subjectively mental – what philosopher Joseph Levine called 'the explanatory gap.'[6] A century of studying the brain provided an impressive and extremely useful science of *correlations*. Researchers learned how to identify the specific brain states associated with recognizing faces, solving problems, feeling pleasure, pain and excitement. Yet the central question remained: Exactly how do physical brain states produce mental ones? In an important sense, the entire endeavor of neuroscience has brought us no closer to understanding this mystery. As the neuroscientist Antonio Damasio remarked in an article for *Scientific American*,

'One question towers above all others in the life sciences: How does the set of processes we call mind emerge from the activity of the organ we call brain?'[7]

Perhaps though, as some argue, consciousness doesn't need explaining, at least not in the way we might expect. If all that exists is matter, and matter is fundamentally without experience, then the subjective heart of consciousness simply cannot be anything more than an illusion. But could this ever serve as a satisfactory conclusion? As early as the 17th century, the philosopher René Descartes observed that the existence of consciousness was the one thing we could never doubt about the universe.[8] The world beyond our senses may be very different to the way our minds perceive it. We could doubt everything we think we know about the outside world. In fact, so corrosive is the acid of Cartesian doubt that it leaves certainty of only a single truth: that I am thinking, that I am conscious. Something, somewhere, is conscious. Descartes subsequently reasoned that mind and matter were two fundamentally different ingredients of the universe – that both were somehow fundamental. Even in his own time, however, others raised concerns with this dualistic view. How could these so different things possibly interact with each other? Could the existence of minds really justify the introduction of a new irreducible element of the universe? For many philosophers, the only tenable starting point for any philosophy is *monism* – a world of one type of stuff. The failure of dualism to satisfy later generations of philosophers led to a general view among thinkers: that mind must be a product of purely physical processes in the brain. Denying the existence of their own experience, many philosophers came to regard the mind as an illusion. But upon whom is this illusion perpetrated? Others have been quick to retort that illusion itself *implies* consciousness. Whatever it is, consciousness is *real*. If it were an *epiphenomenon* – an illusion riding on top of the processes of the brain, by definition it would be powerless to affect any process or perform any function whatsoever. In such thinking, no evolutionary account could explain why it had been preferenced by evolution. If consciousness is just an illusion, how can it *do anything*? There could be no top-down causation going from the mind to the body, let alone the world. Why, then, did natural selection go to all the trouble of providing this rich inner experience of life? Why is the world not populated by what philosophers call 'zombies' – city-building, language-using automata that behave like us in every way, but with 'nobody home'? Consciousness – this flowering of sentience into the universe, as Chalmers has pointed out, is the most mysterious phenomenon ever encountered by science.[9]

THE INTRINSIC CONSCIOUSNESS MOVEMENT

Our standard materialism, as it is commonly understood, is the view that everything that exists is explainable by a complete account of the external physical facts. In 1982, the philosopher Frank Jackson presented his now-famous thought experiment, known as the *knowledge argument*.[10] It illustrated that the existence of consciousness seems to pose a direct challenge to the completeness of materialism. Upon treading beyond the threshold of her black and white room, many philosophers agreed that Mary – the hypothetical color scientist who had never before experienced colors, could not have imagined what they would be like, even though she knew every possible physical fact about brains and the outside world. Mary blinks in disbelief at the rich phenomenal world of color. Nowhere in her detailed knowledge of the wavelengths of light, or the structure of the eye, or the processes of the visual cortex existed the experience of color. It seemed that Mary's knowledge of colors was only complete with the addition of experiential interior qualities, sometimes referred to by philosophers as *qualia*. Jackson's thought experiment suggested that the classical third-person approach of science could not help but leave out the most essential element of the question: the mind that perceives.

We will encounter further looming problems for our standard materialism later in the book, yet despite its apparent inability to account for consciousness, to many thinkers, three centuries of impressively advancing knowledge and technology have cast it as just too big to lose. The philosopher Daniel Dennett assures that consciousness is nothing like the mystery it seems – that experiences are really just processes vying for dominance in the pandemonium of the brain. For Dennett, experiences simply *are* their associated brain processes. Any obvious challenge to this view is to falsely 'pump our intuitions.' Dennett went as far as to say that experiential qualities are illusions, stating, 'There simply are no qualia at all.'[11] Unfortunately, for many of his colleagues, this denial of experience runs up against the same problem as every other materialist theory attempting to explain away consciousness as an illusion: illusions occur *within* consciousness. As neuroscientist and philosopher Sam Harris writes,

> 'To say that consciousness may only seem to exist is to admit its existence in full – for if things seem any way at all, that is consciousness.'[12]

Consciousness is the beginning and end of everything we know about the world. It is, as Descartes pointed out, the one thing that we cannot doubt the full existence of. This remains as true today as it was in the 17th century. There is a real mystery here, and accepting its existence is not a step backwards into superstition or magical thinking, but a step toward firmer footing about what needs to be explained. As we will investigate, academics increasingly recognize the stubborn reality of consciousness as well as the limitations of materialism to account for it. Recent decades have seen the question of consciousness re-enter the mainstream after nearly a century of taboo. The discussion has advanced through a clearer, more modest appraisal of what we know and what we don't. Recognition of the hard problem of consciousness reveals a mysterious blind spot in our scientific understanding of nature, and today a groundswell of leading thinkers are exploring how science may need to expand to include it. Thomas Nagel, a towering figure in contemporary philosophy of mind, had already pointed to an astonishing though potentially unavoidable implication: If it is not possible to explain the subjective aspect of our minds via external physical behaviors and processes, then it cannot be reducible to them. If this is the case, Nagel argued, then consciousness may turn out to be in some way fundamental or *intrinsic* to physics.[13] Chalmers too saw this, arguing that the question of consciousness may go so deep, as to penetrate to the heart of our scientific ontology, with the potential of profoundly reorienting both our views of self and the universe at large.[14] Could it be that the subjective aspect of our minds is an inherent feature of nature, that through complex structures like brains, blossoms into the rich phenomenal landscape of experience? Just as mass and charge are fundamental properties of the particles making up the observed world, might awareness, in some unrefined or proto form, be similarly fundamental? Among thinkers in academia today, there is the growing sense that we have anthropomorphized consciousness, and that its origins lie not in us, but in a deeper aspect of the world. The upsurge of academics supporting deeper views of consciousness constitutes what I will refer to as the *Intrinsic Consciousness movement*. Intrinsic views of consciousness can be found in the thinking of many great historical minds, and many of their ideas remain relevant, and yet in the modern era, in the light of new theories and evidence, intrinsic views of consciousness are now gaining unprecedented traction at the highest levels of academia. The intrinsic consciousness movement embodies many different views and theories arriving from many different disciplines of knowledge. It includes biologists, psychologists, physicists, cosmologists and philosophers. Among their disparate views can be found a common, provocative yet compelling conviction: that a full account of physical reality will require our finding a place for consciousness. It is the belief of this author, that when viewed together, the trend of contemporary ideas point toward a still-coalescing picture of reality, and that while a wide spread shift in thinking may yet lie years ahead of us, we can already begin to glimpse this consciousness-involving reality and see that it is both coherent and defensible. Together we will investigate how this movement not only points toward a richer conception of nature that includes a place for consciousness, but it may also shine light into other deep mysteries in science and philosophy, including, among others, why there is something rather than nothing, why the universe is the way that it is, and what our place is within it. If the intuitions of the intrinsic consciousness movement are correct, and mind reflects something intrinsic about the way reality is organized, this insight will undeniably change how we view ourselves, our relationship to the world and other beings. It could turn out to have far-reaching implications to the values and ethics we live by, even to the way we choose to structure our society and steer it into the future. This view, then, may not only lead to a deeper understanding of the nature of consciousness; it may reveal important and catalyzing insights for our species.

As we trace the intrinsic consciousness movement through different fields, at times the evidence and ideas before us may challenge credulity. In truth, we are taking a big step into the unknown. Yet, given the mysterious nature of the subject matter at hand – the very awakening into awareness of the universe itself – encountering some degree of strangeness will almost certainly be unavoidable if we're to make progress. As David Chalmers warned his audience during a recent *TED talk*, understanding the most mysterious phenomenon ever encountered by science will almost certainly involve entertaining one or two ideas that first sound a little crazy.[15]

Indeed, we'll spend a good deal of time on some pretty far out stuff. It is not my aim to convince you, the reader, that any of these ideas are true, or that any one existing theory is correct. My own thoughts are highly tentative, yet I think that the true nature of things may come as a surprise to everyone. Our aim then, is to hold and examine new ideas and evidence with an open mind. With preconceptions in stow we will tentatively consider the surprising and sometimes-controversial evidence, that beyond our narrow materialism, extraordinary truths await to be known of our situation in being.

WORLD OF MINDS

Parallel to the question of the nature of consciousness is the question of what types of things posses it. Does a dolphin have consciousness? Does a fish? A cell? A photon? We might be certain of our own consciousness, and happily attribute it to other humans, but how can we be sure about other life? Certainly other animals *seem* to have consciousness, displaying behavior indicative of pain, pleasure, fear and excitement. Descartes famously disagreed, a conviction he demonstrated to an incredulous colleague by tossing a passing cat out of his window. For Descartes, who was a religious man, other animals were mere automata – mindless biological robots. Only humans, whom God had endowed with souls, had minds and consciousness. Most pet owners would probably take issue with Descartes here, but if consciousness is not unique to humans, on what other branches of the tree of life does it blossom? For a time it was popular to consider an advanced neocortex to be a prerequisite of consciousness, bestowing the crown of consciousness to privileged human beings alone. Some scientists argued that the higher cognitive abilities evolved for language were the gateway to consciousness. These human-centric confidences were reassessed in 2012 when an international group of world-leading researchers of human and animal sentience convened at Cambridge University to review the progress of their field. While the hard problem of consciousness stubbornly persisted, significant advancements had been achieved. On the basis of hundreds of studies, the scientists agreed that it was no longer possible to deny that many animals engage in intentional behaviors and experience internal affective states. Marking a new consensus in the field, the meeting culminated in the attendees signing what would become known as the *Cambridge Declaration on Consciousness*. It concluded with the following statement:

> 'The weight of evidence indicates that humans are not unique in possessing the neurological substrates that generate consciousness. Non-human animals, including all mammals and birds, and many other creatures, including octopuses, also possess these neurological substrates.'[16]

Do cattle experience the horror of the abattoir? Does the lobster experience being boiled alive in the cauldron? Scientific recognition of the existence of animal sentience supports what many have long suspected: that animals too have the capacity to experience and suffer. Yet this new consensus among scientists is far from trivial. If we can agree that animals consciously experience their lives, can we continue to justify the manner in which humans enslave them? Is it right that animals endure short and unhappy lives so we can consume their bodies when other options are available? This new scientific consensus, now a matter of public record, might yet go some way to enlightening our culture to the ways we brutalize other beings. Changing attitudes toward animal consciousness also forecast a likely implication of all deeper views of consciousness: If consciousness is somehow intrinsic to physics, then minds are almost certainly distributed much more widely throughout nature than we have tended to imagine. This casts light on longstanding moral issues concerning our responsibilities to other life. We may yet approach a view in which consciousness is essentially synonymous with life. Perhaps then, we cannot help but destroy some consciousness in order to sustain our own. Yet even if this is true, there almost certainly exists an oceanic gulf between the consciousness of the vegetable and more complex organisms with brains, nervous systems, and the capacity to self-reflect. If this is the case, on the issue of other life, what may end up mattering more than the presence of consciousness could be its *degree*.

THE EXTENDED MIND

In our journey through the intrinsic consciousness movement we will also explore anomalies of mental phenomena, the mere acknowledgement of which is considered heresy by many scientists. Primarily these anomalies concern the mind's apparent extension in space and time. This evidence falls under the general term *psi*, meaning simply 'of the mind or psyche.' While the mainstream scientific community has long shunned the existence of psi phenomena, the rise of views of consciousness as intrinsic is now leading scientists to look again at this evidence. These effects, observed in both humans and other species, include the apparent exchange of information outside of known sensory channels, the capacity of minds to gain information about events displaced in time and space, and the ability to influence the internal order of sensitive physical systems by intention alone. Collected under rigorously controlled laboratory conditions, this evidence is for the most part very subtle, normally visible only through the application of statistical analysis to large sets of experimental data. The subtle magnitude of these effects, however, should not be confused with a small statistical confidence that they actually exist. As we will explore in later chapters, the cumulative findings of a large number of high quality studies make it no longer tenable to deny the existence of positive psi evidence. Is the scientific establishment justified in their curt dismissal of these effects, the evidence of which appears to meet all the standard criteria of a scientific claim? Some skeptics have recognized that psi experiments indeed *appear* to provide positive evidence, and that modern studies demonstrate high standards of scientific practice. The implications, however, are so radical, so consequential to our most basic assumptions about mind and world, that such global ramifications are considered simply too great to be justified.

But just how extraordinary are psi phenomena? As we will explore, advances in science point to a view of reality that is increasingly accommodating of the space-time 'anomalies' of psi. We live in a world where the space surrounding our bodies is at all times permeated with the information of countless radio stations and websites, where we carry devices in our pockets capable of connecting us instantly with people the other side of the world. Today, deep interconnectivity is recognized as a basic truth of our world, both in terms of our technology, and also in the deep structure of reality as revealed by our most advanced physics. Quantum physics revealed that our world emerges out of a deeply interconnected fabric, and that under certain conditions, this underlying nonlocal order permits different points in space and time to be mysteriously interconnected. The emerging description of nature is decidedly accommodating of psi effects. What remains justifiably controversial is the role of the mind in these phenomena.

As we will begin to investigate in the next chapter, science seems poised to acknowledge that consciousness reflects an intrinsic interior quality of nature. The holistic principles governing physics at more fundamental levels may ultimately require us to recognize that all consciousness is only ever superficially separate. Just as a single gravitational field pervades all space, perhaps our consciousness too reflects a single universal property that is, at its basis, deeply holistic. The natural selection process that brought living organisms into existence has made every available use of the laws of physics, and our fantastic technologies still pale in comparison to the efficiency of Mother Nature. There is no reason to rule out the possibility that life has evolved to take advantage of reality's holistic underpinnings. Should we really be so incredulous of evidence that our conscious minds, which elude all existing scientific methods of capture, are also deeply interpenetrating – and that this becomes most apparent with people we care deeply for, or with events that are highly meaningful to us? Of course, in talking about the evidence of psi, we are not talking about levitating tables with 'supernatural' powers or the tasteless theatrics of television psychics that prey on the emotions of vulnerable individuals and their families. The evidence for psi, as it is presented in scientific papers and journals today, arrives from clinical laboratory studies with stringent controls against mundane factors. Psi may seem almost like magic to us now, and yet nature has historically revealed herself to be richer than our models. On the subject of telepathy, Einstein himself called for open-mindedness when considering psi phenomena.

> 'We have no right to rule out a priori the possibility of telepathy. For that the foundations of our science are too uncertain and incomplete.'[17]

The real challenge of psi comes from what it reveals about consciousness. The theoretical avenues that viably emerge to explain it predominantly involve ascribing some intrinsic experiential aspect to reality itself. In this book we will explore various rationale for considering that consciousness reflects something fundamental about the way reality is organized. If this is true, then psi may turn out to be a natural occurrence – predicted by nature's deeply holistic underpinnings. If psi occurs, then theories of consciousness that fail to make room for it must be subject to radical revision or even abandoned. We, then, had better know for sure if psi is real before we radically alter our theoretical landscape.

I have found some of the existing psi research to be sufficiently compelling to detail some of its findings in this book. For the most part I have avoided the sometimes emotionally charged debates between researchers and self-identified skeptics, which can often appear to create more heat than light. Instead I have favored a more even-handed review of the experiments, the evidence, and what its existence could mean. Scientific progress involves a willingness to closely examine anomalies with an open mind – and never more so than when they concern such deep questions as who we are and our place in the natural order. If even some psi phenomena are real, they necessitate that we turn a page in our journey toward understanding the conscious mind.

Some will challenge my choices of what elements of psi to include in this book. There is no question that the research I have documented represents little more than the tip of the iceberg of a surprising wealth of studies, much of which may carry further important insights. Others will undoubtedly challenge my decision to include this research at all. I have chosen to do so because, having met many of the researchers involved in this field, read their papers, known them as professors and educators, and probed their reasoning in personal interviews, I have found them to be honest, open minded, and above all, highly qualified, diligent scientists. The psi research I have included, to my lights, is free from confounding errors, appearing to reveal important aspects of the nature of consciousness. I cannot, then, in good conscience omit this research from our investigation of the intrinsic consciousness movement. I thus invite you to join me in taking an open-minded approach to these 'anomalies' as we venture into this mysterious terrain. Extraordinary insights may await our discovery. Our investigation into the intrinsic consciousness movement now begins in philosophy, and the rise of deeper views of consciousness.

'Consciousness, however small, is an illegitimate birth in any philosophy that starts without it, and yet professes to explain all facts by continuous evolution. If evolution is to work smoothly, consciousness in some shape must have been present at the very origin of things.' [18]

William James
Father of modern psychology

2. THE INNER LANDSCAPE

Could a new philosophical framework find a place for consciousness without upsetting the elegant ontological economy of monism – a world of one type of stuff? Philosophical enquiry into the question of consciousness has drawn some surprising conclusions, among which is the conviction of several prominent thinkers: that our search for an understanding of consciousness may also lead us to a new understanding of reality.

The view that consciousness is a fundamental aspect of nature is by no means new. In some form, it has been the perspective of almost every human culture recorded to exist on this planet. In fact, it's fair to say that the prevailing modern Western scientific view – that we live in a reality devoid of consciousness, is an exception. As we will explore, there are now modest signs that in Western science and philosophy, attitudes are beginning to shift toward considering a deeper place for consciousness in the natural order. Furthermore, this shift in thinking is occurring at the highest levels of academia.

In recent times, a resurgence of philosophers have argued that there are attractive reasons to consider consciousness exists fundamentally to physics.[1] While seemingly radical, it is a perspective with a rich history in Western philosophy, known as *panpsychism*. In the 17th century, panpsychism was defended by such philosophical luminaries as Baruch Spinoza and Gottfried Wilhelm Leibniz – both influential thinkers of the Enlightenment. In the 19th century, panpsychism was a respectable theory, supported by both philosophers and several prominent early psychologists. Among supporters of panpsychism was the father of the modern psychology, William James. Development of these ideas was curtailed when the philosophical movement of *logical positivism* rose to dominance in the first half of the 20th century, and thinkers became increasingly concerned that philosophy serve as an analytical tool for objective science. A consequence was that introspective and intuitive knowledge were marginalized. In the same period, a similar development was occurring in psychology with the rise of *behaviorism*. With hopes of achieving the status of the 'hard' sciences, psychologists directed the powerful objectivity of empiricism to human behavior. With great ambition, psychologists considered that every datum of the mind could be understood by reduction to environmental inputs and behavioral outputs. For decades, even mentioning consciousness raised eyebrows. Today, however, widening recognition of the hard problem of consciousness has seen panpsychism return as a mainstream theory, with a resurgence of thinkers arguing that only within such a view can we resolve the otherwise miraculous emergence of mind within the physical universe.

But what does it mean to say consciousness is fundamental? What does it mean to say *anything* is fundamental? Space, time, mass and charge are all considered by physicists to constitute fundamental characteristics of nature, governed by fundamental laws. They are so called because they cannot be defined by anything more basic. Historically, the advancement of science has led to the addition of new fundamentals, and with them, the expansion of our scientific picture of the world. One example is electric charge. When, in the 18th century, it was discovered that the existing Newtonian framework couldn't explain electromagnetic phenomena, additional laws were required. Out of this development the property of *charge* emerged as a new fundamental. Might a similar expansion of science be required to explain consciousness? Does some proto-experiential quality exist fundamentally to physics, governed by its own fundamental laws? The challenge for panpsychism is to explain how this intrinsic mind-like quality combines (or fragments) to give rise to experiencing subjects like us. Philosophers disagree about how to resolve this issue, which is known as the *combination problem*. Panpsychism also faces another daunting challenge – it needs to account for *why* something like mentality ought to be located at the foundations of nature in the first place. A fully realized panpsychism would not only explain how minds like ours evolve, it would offer compelling reasons for why physics requires it, and its lawful relationship to observable phenomena.

To understand some of the reasons for the growing popularity of panpsychism, we will familiarize ourselves with a philosophical argument at the heart of many of its new conceptions. It is known as the 'intrinsic nature argument', and despite its recent popularity, elements of the position can be traced to titans of early 20th century philosophy, Bertrand Russell and Arthur Eddington. Its modern form typically begins by taking account of the rich structural description of the world available through scientific observation. It then turns to a concern about the limitation of this description in its ability to capture the 'intrinsic nature' of matter. Before considering what this intrinsic nature may or may not be, let us examine the first claim: that the underlying nature of things lies beyond objective science's ability to grasp.

Science, as we typically conduct it, is an essentially 'third-person' enterprise. While it tells us a great deal about the structural form and tendencies of things, it has no means of penetrating to the essential nature of matter or physical processes as they exist in themselves. Objective science does a very good job of telling us what things and processes *do* but not what they *are*. Take, for example, what science tells us about an electron. An electron has *mass*. Loosely speaking, things with mass attract each other. The electron also has a negative charge – meaning, also very generally, that it will repel other negatively charged particles and attract positively charged ones. The descriptions that physics gives us about the electron are exclusively behavioral – describing only its causal structure. Everything science tells us about the world falls into this single relational category. The underlying *nature* of the electron, and indeed of all reality, is impenetrable by objective science. As Russell points out, 'we know nothing about the intrinsic quality of physical events.'[2] The panpsychist philosopher Alfred North Whitehead described the intrinsic nature of the world as the 'mysterious reality in the background, intrinsically unknowable.'[3]

In spite of its absence from our scientific description of the world, the existence of an intrinsic nature – within which all things are grounded, seems necessary for any full account of reality. Our advancing knowledge of the causal relational structure of nature has permitted us to make powerful predictions and build impressively accurate models of nature. It has given us planes, computers, lasers and cellphones, but in an important respect, the underlying nature of reality remains invisible to objective science. In a particular sense, the problem of the intrinsic nature of the world is analogous to the hard problem of consciousness. We know that it is there, but it resists all attempts to capture it through objective means.

Today a growing number of philosophers believe that the intrinsic qualities underlying physical processes must be characteristically mental or 'phenomenal'. But why do they reason in this way? Surely an inherent limitation of science to grasp reality's intrinsic nature ought to evoke no more than agnosticism toward what it could be? The reason is that inner reflection of our own minds reveals one thing concretely about conscious experience: it is an intrinsic nature. All other objects of science are relational phenomena; everything we know about them is behavioral. Consciousness, on the other hand, we know about directly and without inference. It is, in this respect, a reality in itself. Intriguingly, consciousness is also the only intrinsic nature that we know of. All other apparent candidates, on closer inspection, dissolve into mere tendencies of nature's causal structure. Consciousness, however, is the one thing we cannot doubt the full existence of. The French philosopher Teilhard De Chardin argued that while objective observation grasps the 'world without', only consciousness or sensation can describe the necessary 'world within'. The intrinsic nature of things, what Teilhard called *interiority*, cannot be fully described without recognizing its essentially subjective quality.[4] With its unique imminence, consciousness is like a window, in it and as it, we penetrate to the heart of matter. Today a growing number of philosophers are taking a similar view, arguing that an intrinsic, grounding interiority of matter is a perfect candidate for the otherwise mysterious interiority of minds. Not only is it a possible solution to the hard problem of consciousness, it grounds the physical world in reality while at the same time submitting the necessary vital content to underpin nature's causal structure. Could it be that the intrinsic nature of the world is inherently opaque to objective science for the same reason that our consciousness is: it embodies an essentially subjective quality? It was this reasoning that led Eddington to write,

> 'All through the physical world runs that unknown content, which must surely be the stuff of our consciousness.'[5]

As we saw in the first chapter, Jackson's thought experiment with Mary the color scientist suggested that experiences are a categorically different kind of thing to the brain processes we associate them with. Explaining the intrinsic qualities of experience seems to call for an expansion of our standard picture of nature, and, according to the intrinsic nature argument, physics calls for just the appropriate expansion to accommodate it. The discussion of such intrinsic views of consciousness moves far beyond pre-theoretical concerns that may come to mind about chairs or rocks having minds. Complex minds require the right complex arrangements and processes. Chairs and rocks are aggregates, without a center of integration. Generally speaking, the emerging view is that the processes of physical reality have *interior* topologies as well as the external ones captured by our scientific instruments, and when organized in the appropriate structures, this interior quality of nature underpins the rich inner mental life that beings like us experience. Essentially, the inner nature of the mind is the inner nature of the world. Or put another way, the mental is the physical viewed from within. In philosophy recent years have seen notable contributions in support of this view from David Chalmers, Thomas Nagel, Gregg Rosenberg, Galen Strawson, Freya Mathews, Isabelle Stengers, Torin Alter, Philip Goff, Michael Lockwood, Yujin Nagasawa, William Seager, David Skrbina, Ken Wilber and many others. It is fair to say that in academic philosophy panpsychism is experiencing a new flowering. As British philosopher Philip Goff expressed in a recent radio interview, 'Panpsychism, at this stage of our knowledge, looks to be the most elegant approach of locating a place for consciousness.'[6] Nagel captured the intuitions of this movement in his 2012 book, *Mind and Cosmos,* where he writes,

> 'We ourselves are large-scale complex instances of something, both objectively physical from outside and subjectively mental from inside. Perhaps the basis for this identity pervades the world.'[7]

As we will now explore, in recent years deeper views of consciousness have also gained unprecedented attention in neuroscience.

FOUNDATIONS OF INFORMATION

Philosophers and neuroscientists have long recognized the unity of the mind. While it is the subject of a vast amount of information, our conscious experience is always unified. We cannot, for example, fragment experience by ignoring one side of the visual field or see a shape without its color. Certainly, we could block one eye, or even impair the area of the brain associated with visual perception, and yet our *experience*, whatever its contents, is always a single, unbroken unity. But how do these processes become the subject of a unified experience – an *entity*? This was the question driving neuroscientist Giulio Tononi. Everything about conscious experience is informative. Tononi reasoned that at their most elemental, the contents of consciousness are *informational*. From this starting point he began to consider exactly what it was about the brain's particular informational organization that permits a subjective unified experience. He began investigating what kinds of organization can sustain complex centers of high information. He discovered that systems with high degrees of *integration* have specific qualities not present in other networks. Integrated systems with a large number of bits have a mathematical synergy, the result of which is that any single state serves as a reduction from a large number of other possible states. By way of an example, Tononi asks us to consider a light-sensitive photo diode like those found in a digital camera. A very simple diode might respond to just two states: light or dark. We could present our diode with any number of different images, yet regardless of the picture's content, the diode can respond by assuming just one of two possible states: Is it light, or is it dark? Now imagine yourself looking at the same image. We immediately recognize the image as depicting the sun breaking through morning fog over the San Francisco skyline. For us, perceiving this image results in a reduction from a near infinity of possible states of experience. –Not an image of the Andromeda galaxy, not a childhood picture of your mother, not cells dividing in a Petri dish and so on. Because of the vast number of subjective states we are capable of recognizing, each one is highly informative. In the same way every conscious experience that is distinguishable from others is powerfully informative. Because of the vast number of possible states, our hugely complex and integrated brains permit humans to have a comparatively huge capacity for conscious experience. Where he left behind other mainstream reductionist theories was in his recognition that the property of consciousness itself is irreducible and fundamental. For Tononi, at its very basis information has an intrinsic subjective quality.

The total informational integration of a system can be calculated by a relatively simple mathematical principle Tononi calls 'phi', represented by the Greek symbol, 'Φ'. It describes the total number of possible integrated states the system can assume. Computing phi for the photo diode is easy, but for more complex systems like brains, this value explodes beyond our ability to calculate. Tononi reasoned that a high value of phi present within integrated centers of our brains could be what permits the unified experience of consciousness each of us has. He called his model; *integrated information theory* or IIT.⁸ An important aspect of the theory is that it holds consciousness to be *substrate independent*. In other words consciousness does not depend on brains or biology per se. In fact, IIT predicts that *any* integrated system has a value of phi and thus some degree of consciousness. In this respect IIT aspires to go beyond explaining the correlates of consciousness, to propose an ontological claim about reality; that there is something intrinsically subjective about information itself. But phi is all around us in all sorts of things. All networks of any kind contain integrated information and thus a value of phi greater than zero, even if vanishingly small. According to IIT, every living cell, every electronic circuit, even a proton consisting of just three elementary particles, possesses something, albeit but a glimmer, of awareness. Tononi's theory, then, is a form of panpsychism.

> 'Consciousness is a fundamental property, like mass or charge. Wherever there is an entity with multiple states, there is some consciousness. You need a special structure to get a lot of it but consciousness is everywhere, it is a fundamental property.'⁹

This radical implication of IIT has not turned off leading academics. Since it was first published in 2008, it has steadily gained mainstream interest, with popular articles appearing in *Scientific American*[10] *The New York Times*[11] and *New Scientist*.[12] Christof Koch, who spent fifteen years working alongside Francis Crick on the neurobiological correlates of consciousness, is considered by many to be the world's leading researcher in this field. Koch, who now supports IIT and contributes to its study, openly recognizes that the theory requires us to embrace panpsychism. 'Tononi's theory', he writes, 'offers a scientific, constructive, predictive and mathematically precise form of panpsychism for the 21st century. It is a gigantic step in the final resolution of the ancient mind-body problem.'[13]

IIT has a notable advantage over many of the competing theories of consciousness today. Because it is a mathematical theory, it carries the benefit of being able to make testable predictions. In a series of experiments, Tononi and his colleagues used transcranial magnetic stimulation to send a ripple of activity through the cortex of sleeping participants. The researchers recorded the length of time a ripple of neuronal activity reverberated through the cortex as a measure of its degree of integration. Consistent with the predictions of IIT, they found that ripples of activity sustained significantly longer when individuals were dreaming than during stages of dreamless sleep.[14] When the brain was conscious in the act of dreaming, the cortex had a significantly higher degree of integration.

IIT also predicts the degree of neuronal integration of centers of the brain associated with consciousness, for example why the cortex is so central to consciousness in humans, even though it has far fewer neurons than the cerebellum, which can actually be removed with only minor disruption to consciousness. The reason, IIT holds, is that the neurons of this area are significantly less integrated than those of the cortex. And this is precisely what we find when examining the neural structure of the cerebellum: many more neurons than the cortex, yet much less integration. Tononi envisages that technologies developed to measure neural integration will help determine such questions as whether consciousness exists in unresponsive patients, or the full effectivity of anesthetics. The theory may also shed new light on another contemporary enigma in neuroscience. In cases of individuals suffering from severe epilepsy, an operation is sometimes carried out that splits the *corpus callosum* – the bridge of neural fibers connecting the two hemispheres of the brain. Fragmenting the brain in this way prevents the electrical storms of epilepsy passing from one hemisphere to the other. A surprising result of this operation has been reports of two minds associated with the same brain, capable of very different personalities and desiring very different things.[15] Why this happens is an unsolved mystery in neuroscience, yet Tononi's theory anticipates this outcome, maintaining that an integrated center, divided in the correct manner, will create two integrated centers – two informational 'entities' where only one existed before.

Tononi's theory, right or wrong, carried into modern neuroscience the idea that consciousness is an intrinsic feature of nature. Intrinsic views of consciousness point toward a radical new view of minds: as extensions of the evolving inner psychic dimension of the universe. Koch has also confronted this strange implication, tentatively offering that the universe is mysteriously driven toward the evolution of consciousness. In his 2012 book, *Consciousness – Confessions of a Romantic Reductionist*, he writes,

> 'I do believe that the laws of physics overwhelmingly favored the emergence of

consciousness. The universe is a work in progress. Such a belief evokes jeremiads from many biologists and philosophers but the evidence from cosmology, biology and history is compelling.'[16]

We will return to some of the evidence Koch is referring to here in chapter 10, when we trace the intrinsic consciousness movement through cosmology.

IT FROM BIT

In the mysterious phenomenon of quantum entanglement, a particle in one location can affect another, even though the two are otherwise disconnected in space and time. First predicted by the mathematics of quantum theory, these nonlocal relationships have since been experimentally demonstrated many times under laboratory conditions. Choosing to measure one particle actually defines the properties of its twin. In principle, this will occur even if particles are billions of light years apart. Quantum interconnectedness radically challenged science's long held assumptions about the world. In a mysterious way, all reality is deeply holistic. Quantum physics tells us that, at its most fundamental level, nature stores information *nonlocally*. While it came as a shock to the physics community, entanglement is now an accepted part of the cannon of modern physics. Over the past 50 years physicists have moved progressively toward the view that *information*, rather than matter and energy, lies at the foundations of physics. This understanding was pioneered by physicist John Wheeler, who captured the emerging perspective in his famous aphorism, 'It from bit.'[17] David Chalmers has observed that the movement toward an informational physics is a promising avenue toward a fundamental theory of consciousness. Information seems to carry within it the concept of *meaning*, and so might be understood more completely as having a subjective as well as an objective pole. 'Information', Chalmers wrote, 'is a natural candidate to also play a role in a fundamental theory of consciousness. We are led to a conception of the world on which information is truly fundamental, and on which it has two basic aspects, corresponding to the physical and the phenomenal features of the world.'[18] Might information be the nexus between mind and matter, containing intrinsic aspects of both? Might a richer conception of information, that recognizes both its essentially objective and subjective aspects, be what physicist Wolfgang Pauli predicted when he wrote,

> 'It is my personal opinion that in the science of the future, reality will neither be 'psychic' nor 'physical' but somehow both and somehow neither.'[19]

Information is usually formalized as representing either 'yes' or 'no' – 'one' or 'zero'. In the quantum, we must acknowledge a third state: 'yes *and* no' – 'one *and* zero'. The ability for quantum information to exist in this 'superposition' of multiple states at the same time is what makes quantum computers such an exciting prospect. Quantum computing could potentially make processing times almost instantaneous. Might quantum states employed by the brain help to explain its extraordinary cognitive capacities and seemingly instantaneous processing speeds, perhaps even playing an important role in consciousness? The idea that biological functions of any kind, let alone brains, utilize quantum processes has long been controversial, inciting the scorn of physicists and biologists alike. Recently, however, new evidence has seen attitudes begin to shift.

QUANTUM LIFE

The cells that comprise our bodies seem to operate in their own world of activity and interaction. Life appears, at least superficially, to sit atop the classical order of nature. To what extent, though, is it meaningful that life exists in the larger context of a fundamentally interconnected reality? Are the processes of life detached from reality's holistic underpinnings, or, true to form, has it adapted ways of taking advantage of it? Just a short time ago, the notion of life employing quantum states was met with disbelief in academia. Quantum effects had long been viewed as partitioned from the classical world, reliant on very stable and very cold conditions. This view was challenged in 1999 when researchers at the University of California published a groundbreaking study that revealed photosynthesis – an essential process for life on Earth – was facilitated by cells' ability to martial quantum processes.[20] The team of researchers, led by chemist Graham Fleming, discovered that photons converted into usable energy by the cell were maintained in quantum superposition, sampling all possible paths through the cell simultaneously before settling on the most direct route. It was this that permitted the extraordinary efficiency of photosynthesis – an enduring mystery in biology. As attitudes subsequently began shifting toward the possibility of quantum processes in life, other studies began locating them elsewhere. The inner compass of migrating birds – used to detect the orientation of the electromagnetic field of the planet – was discovered by researchers to be influenced by radio waves. This interference was completely unanticipated by the prevailing theories of how this sense operated, revealing the telltale signs that quantum processes were involved.[21] A later independent study revealed that the sense of smell, common to many species, was just too sensitive to be explained by the dominant theory, in which passing molecules connected like *Lego* to molecular receptor sites. Fruit flies were discovered to be able to tell the difference between hydrogen and deuterium, even though their atomic structures are chemically identical. The only difference was a quantum one: a single extra neutron in the nucleus of the deuterium atom. The conclusion was that this sense relied on organisms employing quantum states here too.[22] Today it seems increasingly likely that we will continue to identify quantum states in new biological processes. In an article for *Nature* in 2011, the chemist and popular science writer Philip Ball reflected that an entirely new understanding of biology could await us in the quantum.[23] So what about the mind? With quantum processes now a growingly accepted part of life's repertoire, it seems at least possible that brains – the most complex structures in the known universe – might also employ them. As several physicists have pointed out, consciousness seems to carry qualities not unlike those identified in the quantum. Might entanglement between brain processes explain the mysterious unbroken unity of consciousness? As physicist Werner Heisenberg remarked,

> 'The same organizing forces that have shaped nature in all her forms are also responsible for the structure of our minds.'[24]

Before the modern advances in quantum biology, in 1996, physicist Roger Penrose and anesthesiologist Stuart Hameroff proposed a theory of consciousness that relied on the existence of quantum processes occurring in the brain.[25] Their theory, *Orchestrated Objective Reduction*, also known as 'Orch-OR', as well as making the then controversial claim that quantum processes were not entirely irrelevant to life, also proposed the existence of a form of panpsychism. Orch-OR was developed from Hameroff's observation, that the scaffolding-like filaments present in all cells, known as *microtubules*, carry the precise structure necessary to act like tiny quantum computers. These quantum effects, as well as permitting nonlocal coherence between different regions of the brain, bridged these processes with an inherent 'proto-conscious' quality of the fine-scale structure of the universe. While the two scientists continued to stand by their theory, others continuously attacked it in academia. This was largely due to their incredulity that quantum processes could be maintained in the warm, wet environment of the brain without quickly being destroyed by quantum decoherence. It wasn't until 2013 that the contentious issue of whether microtubules could sustain quantum effects was resolved. Researchers at Japan's *National Institute for Materials Science*, led by molecular biologist and physicist Anirban Bandyopadhyay, discovered quantum effects could indeed be maintained within microtubules.[26] Furthermore, these quantum states were also shown to sustain within the threshold of time required by Penrose and Hameroff's theory.

If quantum processes are involved in consciousness, one of the unsettling implications is that it may carry some of the strange and counterintuitive features of quantum systems. Many physicists and neuroscientists remain cautious of quantum approaches to consciousness because, unless they can be shown with certainty, quantum states involved in consciousness may unnecessarily render the hard problem of consciousness even more mystifying. One thing does seem evident: quantum mechanics alone cannot explain consciousness. It is essential to explain *why* any particular physical process, quantum or otherwise, should be accompanied with subjective experience. At some future time quantum processes may be shown to explain how different regions of the brain contribute to a unified experience, and yet understanding *why* this quantum unity of processes gives rise to an inner subjectivity reencounters the hard problem, only now with the addition of strange quantum effects. Quantum physics may indeed be necessary to understand consciousness, but the 'hard problem' still seems to require we attribute some form of mental quality to nature itself. Indeed, Penrose and Hameroff agreed, maintaining that a form of panpsychism would be necessary to truly understand consciousness. If the experiential really does have its roots in a deeper order of reality, a reasonable prediction is that our minds are subject to the same nonlocal principles governing fundamental levels of nature. If so our minds may not be as confined to our brains as we have tended to suppose.

Beyond the holistic underpinnings of reality revealed by quantum nonlocality, physicists also encountered another profound enigma at the very heart of the quantum. Many physicists, including the founders of quantum theory, have argued that we will ultimately need to confront this enigma in order to unlock the mystery of sentience. We now enter deeper into the strange world of quantum physics, where a century-old debate still rages over the role of conscious observers in the establishment of physical reality itself.

'All ideas we form of the outer world are ultimately only reflections of our own perceptions. Can we logically set up against our self-consciousness a 'Nature' independent of it?' [27]

Max Planck
Father of quantum theory

3. MIND AND MATTER

In academic circles today connecting consciousness with findings in modern physics is undoubtedly controversial. Physicists choosing to talk openly on the subject risk loosing the respect of their peers and even jeopardizing their career. While this may be unfair, there is valid reason for caution when venturing into this area. In popular writing there is no shortage of examples of the misuse of quantum physics, which is often employed to appropriate legitimacy to New Age and spiritual concepts. Surprisingly though, some of the comparisons between spiritual ideas and the new physics were first drawn by quantum physicists themselves. Niels Bohr, Erwin Schrödinger and Wolfgang Pauli each turned to Eastern contemplative philosophies in an attempt to make sense of the strange and interconnected world described by quantum theory. Texts like the *Vedas* and the *Yoga Sutras* were grounded in similarly holistic principles hailed by the new physics and some considered whether centuries of thinking in these terms had yielded insights applicable to the questions with which they were now grappling.

In recent decades, the popularity of connecting quantum mechanics to metaphysical and spiritual concepts has led to the rise of what is sometimes known as *quantum mysticism*. While some of these parallels are compelling and worthy of interest, today an entire culture has grown out of quantum mysticism and many scientists are cautious of its potential to mislead. Beyond the interconnected reality it describes, there is no aspect of quantum physics more controversial than the discovery that the kinds of questions we pose to nature play a mysterious role in the way it presents itself. While this finding is ripe for misappropriation, as we will now explore, the question of the possible importance of consciousness in quantum mechanics remains an open one. The new physics revealed an apparent relationship between mind and world, so unexpected, that it radically changed the worldviews of those physicists that discovered it. The founder of quantum theory, Max Planck, became convinced that consciousness was intrinsic to all of reality. In his own words,

> 'I regard consciousness as fundamental. I regard matter as derivative from consciousness. We cannot get behind consciousness. Everything that we talk about, everything that we regard as existing, postulates consciousness.'[1]

Another important contributor to quantum theory, Eugene Wigner, reflected,

> 'It was not possible to formulate the laws of quantum mechanics in a fully consistent way

without reference to the consciousness. The very study of the external world led to the conclusion that the content of consciousness is the ultimate reality.'[2]

The significance of consciousness in quantum physics can also be found explicitly in the writings of Erwin Schrödinger,[3] Pascual Jordan,[4] John von Neumann[5] and Wolfgang Pauli[6] – all of whom made important contributions to the development of quantum theory. But what led them to think this way? Are they, as their modern day critics believe, dead wrong? And if they are, what encouraged leading physicists to stand by such a radical position? The consciousness-involving interpretations of Planck and his contemporaries are sometimes attributed to their naivety of a new and unintuitive physics. While in modern times a taboo has grown around connecting quantum physics with anything mental, we will explore why a number of respected scientists continue to stand by the view that a more complete understanding of quantum physics will require the recognition of a fundamental role of consciousness. In their book documenting a century of advances in quantum physics, physicists Bruce Rosenblum and Fred Kuttner argued that on-going advances, rather than deflating the position, have only lent support for consciousness-involving interpretations.[7] Such a role for observers would entail that mind is more than a passive feature of the universe – that it is in someway intimately involved in the process of reality. So, what is the justification for this radical and hotly debated view?

THE MYSTERY OF MEASUREMENT

To their surprise, physicists discovered that the outcomes of quantum experiments seemed to depend on the types of questions they chose to ask. Run an experiment one way and particles behave like tiny objects, traveling a distinct path with defined properties. Run the experiment another way, and particles behave like waves of potential, occupying multiple states and traveling multiple paths simultaneously. Mysteriously, the outcome of such experiments seems to depend inextricably on the information that can be made available to observers. Prior to observation, the quantum world exists in a flux of potentiality, without standard classical properties. However, we never see the world this way. It seems that when we attempt to gain information about the path a particle takes through a quantum system, the very act of measurement collapses its probabilistic state into distinct properties. This enigma is known as the *quantum measurement problem* (QMP) and it presents itself at the forefront of all quantum experiments.

The mystery of the QMP is perhaps most clearly demonstrated in what physicists call the *double-slit experiment*. First conceived to test the wave-like nature of light, it reveals both the dualistic nature of sub-atomic particles – to behave as either objects or waves, and the apparent role of an observer's choices in which of these behaviors they assume. In the double-slit experiment, light is beamed toward two tiny holes or 'slits' in a barrier. Light passing through the slits encounters a sensitive detector screen that registers where it collides. If light acts like discrete physical particles, commonsense predicts that the pattern left by those particles making it through the slits and onto the detector screen will resemble two clusters of impact points directly behind the two slits. However, when we conduct the experiment, the results show that light actually behaves like a wave, producing a ripple-like interference pattern of bright and dark bands on the screen. This is at first baffling because physicists know that light is comprised of discrete physical packets of energy: particles they call *photons*. Furthermore, in the double-slit experiment it is also possible to reduce the illumination of the light source until just a single photon is emitted at a time. Even under this condition, however, repeatedly directing single photons toward the slits produces the same wave-like effect, with an interference pattern gradually developing on the detector screen. This retrospectively reveals that the photons in fact travelled through the slits more like a cloud of potential, without distinct physical properties. It is as if the individual photons went through both slits simultaneously and interacted with themselves. The mystery deepens further when we attempt to determine exactly which way a photon travelled through the slits. When we attempt to gain information about the photon's path by placing detectors at the slits, they no longer behave as waves, now acting like tiny particles – traveling a single path, going through either one or neither of the slits. Now the pattern on the screen conforms to the way we might expect individual particles to behave – clustering together on the screen directly behind each of the slits. Our gaining access to information about the photons' path mysteriously alters their behavior. This surprising result occurs the same way every time the experiment is conducted.

So, how exactly does the QMP relate to the choices of observers? We will now consider three hypothetical experiments that clarify, in simple terms, the apparent link between the choices made by observers and the way reality presents itself. First conceived by Rosenblum and Kuttner, these thought experiments are simplified demonstrations for non-physicists.[9] Keep in mind that, while simplified, each of these experiments portrays undisputed and independently demonstrable principles of quantum physics.

THREE THOUGHT EXPERIMENTS

Recall the double-slit experiment, but now, instead of having two slits in a single barrier, an experimenter presents us with two boxes, each containing a closed slit facing a detector screen. All we are told at the beginning of the experiment is that there is just one photon, which we naturally assume to be occupying one of the two boxes. In this first experiment, the experimenter asks us to determine which box the photon is inside by opening them one at a time, waiting for an indication that the particle has collided with the detector screen. We quickly learn that, if after opening the first slit and no photon registers on the detector screen, we can know for sure that it will be in the second box. Sure enough, when we conduct the experiment this way, the photon always reveals itself to have been in one box and not the other. We do this experiment again and again, allowing the photons to collide with the detector screen and a visible pattern to develop. Looking at the screen we can see that the photons behaved as tiny classical objects like marbles, with their impact points clustering together directly in line with the boxes from which they arrived. We comfortably conclude that the photon was always located inside only one of the boxes – just as we might expect. Nothing too surprising so far.

We now move to the second experiment, in which we are provided with two boxes organized in the same arrangement. Here, we get our first glimpse of quantum strangeness. This time we are told to open both of the slits simultaneously. The consequence of opening the slits this way is that now we cannot know from which box the photon has arrived. When we do this multiple times, to our surprise, the pattern developing on the screen no longer indicates that the photons behaved as classical objects, instead producing an interference pattern indicative that the photons had behaved like a wave. The only logical conclusion we can draw is that the photon has mysteriously occupied *both* boxes at the same time (known as a distributed wave-function). The experimenter now prompts us to repeat the experiment several more times, each time moving the boxes slightly further apart. The result is that on the screen there now develops a *series* of wave signatures that correspond to the varying distances between the boxes when the slits were opened. From this we learn that the distance between the boxes corresponds to the distribution of the wave signature. In other words, the principle governing where the photons collide with the screen is always determined by the position of *both* boxes. This would be impossible if the photon had really been wholly inside just one box.

Our experimenter now reminds us of the first experiment – where we opened the slits one-at-a-time to determine which box the photon had been inside. Here we were satisfied that the photon had, in fact, always been wholly inside just one of the boxes. In the second experiment, though, where we couldn't know which box the photon was inside, it seemed to have been distributed between *both*. This is strange, but we had concluded to ourselves that this was simply just the way the boxes were prepared by the experimenter. The experimenter then reveals that there is a third and final experiment. We are once again given two boxes. This time we are told we can freely choose either to open the two boxes one-at-a-time (as in the first experiment) or simultaneously (like the second experiment). Now, when we check to see which box the photon comes out of, we find that it was located wholly in one of the boxes, but when we don't, it behaves like a wave of probability, seemingly occupying both boxes. It is now we realize the surprising truth: there is nothing special about the way the experimenter had prepared the boxes – we can actually *choose* how the particles were distributed between them depending on whether we decide to observe or not. We find ourselves asking, 'what was really going on inside the boxes before we made our decision?' Our seemingly arbitrary choice, either to look or not, appears to somehow travel backwards in time, defining the distribution of the photon between the boxes *before* we opened the slits. Not only does observing the photon resolve its properties, it also seems to mysteriously resolve its past. Here, quantum mechanics presents us with a bizarre ultimatum: either reality has deterministically conspired to always present itself in a way that correlates with our choices to observe, or our observations themselves define it. These findings are so inconsistent with our familiar ways of thinking about matter and of an objectively real world separate from our observations that they seem to necessitate an understanding of reality in which observation itself is fundamental. As Pascual Jordan once famously commented,

> 'Observations not only disturb what has to be measured, they produce it. We compel the electron to assume a definite position. We ourselves produce the results of the measurement.'[10]

THE SUBJECTIVE WORLD

A role for observers in quantum mechanics not only challenges the view that consciousness is an isolated illusion of brains; it also challenges the first principles upon which science is based. Since the inception of science, it has progressed by routinely removing all trace of the subjective from nature. This is what allows us to gather independently verifiable evidence and build objective models based on the behavior of the world. This premise rests at the very heart of the standard experimental method. Quantum physics seems to reveal that at the deepest level of nature to which we can currently probe, a purely objective science becomes impossible. The trusted concept of *realism* – of a physically real world independent of observation and measurement, can no longer serve as an ultimate description of reality. Instead, this view becomes relegated to a convenient, though incomplete way of thinking about nature. We have much for which to thank the objective approach of science, and technologies developed from it will continue to advance our species long into the future, yet in our deeper search to understand the true nature of reality, we may need to recognize that our own subjectivity reflects something intrinsic about the world. As Max Planck wrote,

> '[Objective] science cannot solve the ultimate mystery of nature. And that is because, in the last analysis, we ourselves are part of nature and therefore part of the mystery that we are trying to solve.'[11]

Over the last century many in academia have pushed back against these disconcerting findings, which seem to contest objective science's dominion over nature. Claiming to understand quantum mechanics is a regrettable gaffe in any academic circle. As Richard Feynman once confidently stated, 'I can safely say that nobody understands quantum mechanics.'[12] Recognizing the *mystery* at its heart, however, is possible by anyone willing to look closely at the experiments. While ignoring the apparent encounter between quantum mechanics and consciousness has become standard practice among professional physicists, many are increasingly willing to confront it. Today, interpretations of quantum mechanics favoring a fundamental significance of consciousness are supported by many leading physicists, including among others, Paul Davies,[13] Bernard d'Espagnat,[14] Freeman Dyson,[15] Roger Penrose,[16] Henry Stapp[17] and Andrei Linde.[18] Despite consciousness-involving interpretations being considered by reputable scientists, there are also numerous competing interpretations that do not include consciousness at all. In Hugh Everett's *'many worlds'* interpretation, our observations always find us in one of the many branches of the wave function. In other words, the particle never collapses from its probabilistic state. Every single possible eventuality of where the particle could end up really happens *somewhere*. Essentially, in every moment the universe branches into untold trillions of different worlds. For the explanation to really work these cannot simply be abstract, probabilistic worlds, they must be granted full reality. There is a real, existing world where you never picked up this book, where your mother never met your father, where the sun never formed and a near infinity of variations of every conversation, event, possible history and resulting outcome occur. There is a real and existing world where you win the maximum lottery every single week. It is certainly possible, at least in principle, that the many worlds interpretation is true, and some scientists argue that we ought simply to accept it, yet it also seems to be the limit case for believability. An infinite landscape of other worlds is a compelling and exciting idea, and it makes for great science fiction, but is it really the explanation for why our choices seem to influence the way the quantum world behaves? It is surely no less incredible than the idea that consciousness may be involved. In spite of being favored by early pioneers of quantum theory and still many physicists today, consciousness-involving interpretations remain controversial. Some detractors have criticized connecting consciousness with quantum physics as just the 'mixing of mysteries.' In response to this charge, the quantum physicist Henry P. Stapp has replied,

> 'Quantum approaches to consciousness are sometimes said to be motivated simply by the idea that quantum theory is a mystery and

> consciousness is a mystery, so perhaps the two are related. That opinion betrays a profound misunderstanding of the nature of quantum mechanics, which consists fundamentally of a pragmatic scientific solution to the problem of the connection between mind and matter.'[19]

Another thinker who has thought deeply on the relationship between consciousness and the quantum is philosopher David Chalmers. He points out that the observer-involving physics revealed by quantum mechanics seems to be precisely the kind necessary to preserve an active role for consciousness. He identifies the hard problem of consciousness and the quantum measurement problem as perhaps the two most mysterious metaphysical issues we face, and argued that there are compelling reasons to consider they are deeply connected.

> '...if one was to design elegant laws of physics that allow a role for the conscious mind, one could not do much better than the bipartite dynamics of standard quantum mechanics.'[20]

Chalmers observes that one of the principle reasons scientists reject any role of consciousness is on grounds that there doesn't seem to be any room at the foundations of physics for these proposed additional mental forces. He points out that, with quantum mechanics, this is simply no longer the case. In the quantum measurement problem there is revealed what he describes as 'a giant causal opening that is perfectly suited for consciousness to fill.' [21] Schrödinger's famous equation describes the unmeasured quantum world as in a state of superposition. The question is; what collapses this flux of possibilities into the distinct actualities of the world we see around us? Chalmers denotes the term 'M property' ('M' standing for measurement) to that which causes the quantum wave function's collapse. Exactly what it is that plays the role of 'M property' remains an open question. He argues that consciousness is a viable if controversial candidate for the M property, and offers several attractive reasons why we might consider it. Firstly, a central feature of an M property that is necessary for it to perform the role of collapse is that it cannot itself exist in a state of superposition. Chalmers observes that the same seems true of consciousness. It seems to be inconceivable to imagine a superposition of consciousness. Our experience of consciousness always exists as a unity. 'You might take it that it is the very nature of consciousness that it cannot exist in a superposed state.' If so, entangled potentialities would always collapse when realized within some consciousness. Chalmers also observes that consciousness already appears to play an obvious role in the world; we make choices apparently beginning in consciousness that lead to physical actions in the world. Reductionist theories that make consciousness an illusion have a hard time explaining how mind and consciousness can affect physical changes in the body let alone in the world. But if consciousness is not an illusion, and instead is a fundamental property, as Chalmers maintains, then perhaps it plays the causal role it appears to. Another attractive reason to consider consciousness as the M property is that a connection between consciousness and measurement gives an intuitively satisfying clarification for the idea of measurement. 'It's very natural for us to consider measurement as conscious perception.' Viewing consciousness as the M property provides an intelligible explanation for why we never observe the world as a superposition. If consciousness is fundamental and irreducible, as Chalmers believes, then its performing the function of measurement provides this fundamental property with a fundamental role to play.

Chalmers admits to a few potential problems with his argument, the most serious of which he identifies as the independently mysterious *quantum Zeno effect*, which is the finding that an unstable particle, if continuously observed, will never decay. In these instances, continuous observation apparently freezes the evolution of a quantum system. Whether or not we are convinced that consciousness plays a role in measurement, or frustrated by vague and unscientific interpretations, it is clear that the issue is far from resolved. Later, in chapter 10, we trace the intrinsic consciousness movement through cosmology, where we find highly respected physicists arguing that what we have called 'consciousness' may represent a necessary self-reflective principle, intrinsically involved in the evolution of the entire universe. We now turn to a recent series of experiments specifically designed to explore the role of consciousness in quantum measurement. The unorthodox approach of these experiments, as we will now investigate, has led to extraordinary findings.

'The doctrine that the world is made up of objects whose existence is independent of human consciousness turns out to be in conflict with quantum mechanics and with facts established by experiment.' [22]

Bernard d'Espagnat
Quantum physicist

4. ANOMALOUS OBSERVATIONS

The role of measurement in quantum mechanics has been widely discussed in the mainstream literature and many physicists have weighed in on this enduring enigma. Despite a continued interest in consciousness-involving interpretations, there have been almost no experiments directly exploring this possibility. That was, until relatively recently. In 2008, psychologist Dean Radin published the results of an unorthodox new experiment.[1] His study, conducted at the *Institute of Noetic Sciences* (**IONS**) in Northern California, was designed to remove all external variables other than the possible influence of an observer's attending mind. The results were striking. Not only were participants apparently able to influence a quantum system without any direct physical contact, distinct psychological factors were also discovered to play an important role.

Radin realized that any study attempting to directly explore the influence of an observer's attention would essentially be classed as a psi experiment. The psi literature contains many studies investigating the possibility of mind-matter interaction. While they remain controversial, Radin's prior experiences conducting research in this field made him open-minded about the possible efficacy of this approach. In these new experiments, participants would essentially be asked to observe a quantum system *psychically*.

For these experiments, which required an ability to direct continuous attention toward a target, it made sense to use individuals with some prior skill. Meditation, it occurred to Radin, is an exercise that in almost all forms serves as an effective means of attentional training. He elected to use both participants with no attentional training as well as long-term meditators – some with 20 or more years of experience. One of his predictions then, was that the meditators would achieve more success than those participants without any specific attentional training.

In creating the standard conditions for quantum measurement, Radin decided to use an instrument called a *Michelson interferometer*. Just as in the classic double-slit experiment, photons directed through an interferometer can travel two possible paths. Instead of slits, the interferometer has a half-silvered mirror that directs photons toward either one of two other mirrors. Both of these mirrors then direct the photons towards a detector screen. When the path of the photons is not resolved by measurement, they appear to traverse both paths simultaneously as a wave, causing an interference pattern to develop on the screen. Determining their path, which can be done by simply blocking one of the mirrors, results in a particulate signature replacing the interference pattern.

In exploring a consciousness-involving interpretation of measurement, Radin wanted to see if participants could reduce the interference pattern of photons simply by the act of directing their attention to them.

In experimental sessions, he instructed his participants to quiet their minds to a focused state of attention. Using their own mental strategy, they would then direct their attention toward the interferometer and attempt to 'observe' the incoming photons. Participants were located in a separate room to the instrumentation, which was inside an electromagnetically shielded chamber, with careful controls against any temperature fluctuation or vibration in the instrument's environment. With this arrangement, Radin sought to exclude any possible variable other than, perhaps, the participant's attention. 'The task is very simple', he remarked during a conference presentation, 'we tell people where to put their mind and *gain* information.'[2] The experimental sessions consisted of a series of thirty-second trials, during which the participants focused their minds toward the photons, specifically to those traveling through one of the arms of the interferometer. The same number of control trials is also run, in which participants relaxed their attention and associated elsewhere. The results of his first series of experiments were compelling, providing tentative evidence that, by directing their attention towards the photons, participants were indeed reducing the interference pattern and to a statistically significant degree. He calculated the probability of these results occurring due to chance at approximately 500 to one.[3] Just as expected, in the control sessions, where trials were collected unattended, results came out at chance. This was a promising sign that the effect was not due to mundane environmental factors. The really interesting results, however, were revealed when the trials of experienced meditators were contrasted with those of the untrained participants. When he partitioned the data in this way, untrained participants were revealed to have had almost no measurable effect on the interference pattern, producing results very close to chance. The results of the meditators, on the other hand, were associated with odds against chance of 107,000 to 1. Radin was astonished. These were exactly the results he had been hoping for. For most participants the difficulty of the task had been surprising. Significant effort was required to maintain attention for any period of time, and for most people, was possible only for fleeting moments. Try as they might, participants complained that their minds endlessly strayed from the task at hand. The experienced meditators, however, approached the experiment with years of attentional training, and proved highly capable of directing and maintaining their attention toward a single focus. If the results had been an artifact – no more than some error in the experimental design or instrumentation – there should have been no difference whatsoever between the results of the two groups. Any potential problem with the design of the experiment should have impacted both groups the same way. The only feasible remaining explanation, Radin tentatively offered, was that the results showed what they appear to: the minds of his participants were somehow influencing the photons traveling through the interferometer, causing them to behave in a more particulate way.

In 2012, Radin and five associate researchers submitted a paper to the journal *Physics Essays* detailing a further series of experiments.[4] For this new study they had decided to use a classic double-slit arrangement, directing photons via a low powered laser toward two tiny holes in a barrier. A highly sensitive digital camera captured and recorded the interference pattern. The entire apparatus was shielded within a precision-machined light-tight aluminum housing, and as before, controls ensured that temperature fluctuations or vibrations within the environment did not affect the apparatus. Any reduction of the interference pattern could be interpreted via a measured drop in the maximum illumination occurring across the pixels of the digital camera.

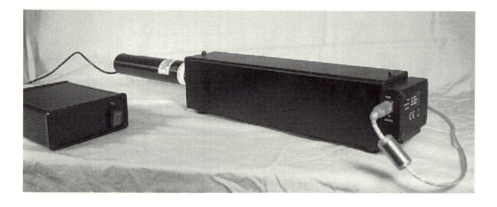

This image shows (from the left) the regulated power supply for the laser and the laser tube, extending beyond the aluminum shielding that surrounds the double-slit apparatus.

Their report listed two primary assumptions of the study, which were as follows:

ASSUMPTION A

> If information is gained – by any means – about a photon's path as it travels through two slits, then the quantum wavelike interference pattern, produced by photons traveling through the slits, will 'collapse' in proportion to the certainty of the knowledge obtained.[5]

ASSUMPTION B

> If some aspect of consciousness is a primordial, self-aware feature of the fabric of reality, and that property is modulated by us through capacities we enjoy as attention and intention, then focusing human attention on a double-slit system may extract information about the photon's path, and in turn that will affect the interference pattern.[6]

As with the previous study, these new experiments drew from two distinct participant populations – one consisting of ordinary participants, the other consisting of individuals with years of meditative practice. Once again, participants were asked to direct their attention toward the apparatus and attempt to remotely observe the photons.

In their report, the researchers detailed the findings of six new experiments, in which they had modified features of the original experiment in an attempt to explore different aspects of this mysterious effect. Intriguingly, their results appeared to confirm Radin's previous finding: meditators were significantly better at reducing the interference pattern than untrained participants. As before, in control trials – where no attention was directed toward the photons – no significant reduction in the interference pattern occurred.

One experiment attempted to test a mysteriously timeless aspect of observation. Among the most baffling implications of quantum theory is that an observation of a quantum system can occur at *any* time. For example, choosing to measure a photon in the present seems to resolve how it behaved in the past. It is as though the act of measurement produces histories that are consistent with the present choice to observe. As the physicist John Wheeler once famously remarked, '*We* decide what the photon *shall have done* after it has already done it.' [7] The IONS researchers now designed an experiment to see if their effect followed the same principle. The results indeed suggested that it did. Participants could apparently reduce the interference pattern even when their attempts were directed toward unobserved trials that had been recorded *two months previously*. Furthermore, their results were also very similar in magnitude to trials conducted in real time. Participants in the present indeed seemed to be resolving how the photons had behaved in the past. Strangely, while the effect appeared to transcend the familiar constraints of time, in another of their experiments, where electrodes were placed on participants' scalps during trials, brain activity indicative of focused attention was found to positively correlate with times when the interference pattern was reduced.

Taking stock of these surprising findings, the researchers decided to calculate the results of their four previous experiments using a double-slit. Both control sessions and those with untrained participants had produced results very close to chance. Meditators continued to produce positive results with odds against chance of 13,800 to 1. Following these encouraging results, the researchers elected to conduct a further 50-session study. This time, the experiment used only participants predicted to perform well. Staggering results were obtained, this time associated with odds against chance of 268,000 to 1. The mysterious role of observation in quantum mechanics might indeed involve a psychic component.

In the final experiment of their report, the researchers decided to test the extent to which participants' belief in the possibility of psi played a role in their ability to produce effects. This was motivated by previous findings in the psi literature that identified psychological openness to psi phenomena as predictive of larger effects. In their experiment they selected a varied population of individuals holding a wide range of beliefs. They didn't anticipate large effects overall, instead they simply tested to what extent – if any, openness to psi phenomena would be predictive of participants' results. It was. Individuals reporting openness to psi tended to produce more robust effects than other participants.

By the following year, Radin and three colleagues had devised a way to carry out the experiment over the Internet.[8] Logging on to a website, people from all around the planet could now attempt to influence a quantum system located at the IONS laboratory in Northern California. Some five thousand participants contributed sessions from all around the world. Their distances from the double-slit apparatus ranged from four to eighteen thousand kilometers. In these experiments, a participant logged onto a website, where they carried out a series of eleven-minute sessions, each consisting of 21 distinct periods. Control sessions were generated by a software robot, which carried out all the actions taken by a participant during an experimental session, only without anyone present. Some seven thousand of these automated sessions were run. The overall results of these control periods remained safely within that anticipated by chance. Trials involving participants, however, produced highly compelling results overall. Just as with previous experiments, analysis was conducted on the degree of *fringe visibility* of the interference pattern. The results suggested that, even from thousands of miles away, participants were somehow influencing the quantum system.

So how exactly does the attending mind reach out beyond the brain and body? If the relationship is sustained via some signal, perhaps emanating from the participant's brain, we might expect an increasing 'drop off' in the effect at greater and greater distances. However, just as many other studies appear to show, psi effects, subtle as they may be, do not drop off whatsoever over space, at least not across the local distances available for study. Regardless of where in the world participants submitted their online trials, the overall magnitude of effect was approximately the same. The relationship seemed appropriately termed 'nonlocal'. Like the imminent relationship between distant entangled particles, the observer's attention and the photons seem engaged in an intimate dialogue, unbound by space. The implications are challenging. If the effect really *is* nonlocal, then the attending mind of an observer is potentially intimately interrelated with the entire universe. The findings of these experiments not only support a role for consciousness in quantum measurement, and thus a participatory role for minds in the physical universe; they defy any reductive materialist theory of mind. The results of these ongoing experiments suggest that the mind extends beyond the skull in ways that apparently transcend or precede space and time. This might be much harder to believe were it not for an extensive published psi research literature featuring the same extended characteristics of mind under different experimental conditions. We will explore what I consider to be some of the most reliable and insightful of that research in coming chapters. The subjective heart of consciousness continues to resist science's characteristically objective approach, yet as we will investigate, psi experiments may reveal subtle traces of mind visible in its wake. It is through investigation of these mysterious traces that psi researchers have been able to make astonishing inferences about the nature of consciousness.

5. CONSCIOUSNESS AS AN ORDERING PRINCIPLE

Among the first experiments exploring mind-matter interaction were conceived by parapsychologists in the early 20th century. They explored the possibility that consciousness may act as a form of ordering principle in the physical world. These early studies were crude by today's standards, but researchers such as **J.B Rhine** of Duke University reported compelling evidence of effects. When directed toward labile physical processes such as dice throws, the directed intention of ordinary participants seemed to subtly shift outcomes to a statistically significant degree. While his work drew many interested supporters, many in the scientific community regarded Rhine's research with hostility and skepticism. His critics, who often refused even to look at his data, accused him of not properly controlling for possible confounding variables, even suggesting that he deliberately falsified his data. No evidence of fraud has ever been found.

So was there anything to these early experiments? In the 1970s Helmut Schmidt, a German-born physicist working for the Boeing aircraft manufacturer, had become intrigued by the possibility of mind-matter interaction. To test the validity of Rhine's assertions, he decided to repeat his mind-matter experiments using the more sophisticated technology of his day. The psi literature credits Schmidt with the development of one of the early truly random event generators (REG). Essentially REGs are instruments that produce a binary stream of data that draws from a truly random process. Sometimes called a 'maximum entropy system' an REG essentially performs the electronic equivalent of flipping a coin. Schmidt's instrument derived its random process from the individual release of electrons from a small piece of weakly radioactive material – an inherently probabilistic quantum event. Using his REG, Schmidt designed a series of experiments to explore a possible mind-matter interaction effect. In his classic experiment the REG output was converted into a circle of electronic lights that moved in a clockwise or anti-clockwise direction. He asked his participants to focus on the lights and attempt to influence them to move in a pre-stated direction. Results were recorded by an automatic print readout from the instrument. Not only were these studies more precise than Rhine's earlier experiments, where data had been recorded by hand, significantly more data could now be acquired in much less time. It was clear early on that this effect, if it existed, was extremely subtle, and statistical measures would be needed to identify it. Statistics is a powerful analytic tool used widely in science. It allows researchers to identify effects that might otherwise be hidden amongst the 'noise' of large sets of data. If an effect is real, yet very subtle, it could be overlooked in just a few trials. If multiple trials are run however, random or idiosyncratic fluctuations should gradually 'wash out.' The effect, if there is one, should become visible in bold relief. In Schmidt's experiments, distinguishing between the 'signal' of a possible psi effect and the 'noise' of ordinary random fluctuations meant carrying out many hundreds of trials and diligently collecting and recording all data.

His results were intriguing. When subject to a participant's intention, the ordinary random behavior of the REG indeed seemed to change – no longer behaving randomly, with very small though significant increments of statistical order occurring in line with the participants' pre-defined intentions.[2] When they intended the lights to go to the right or to the left, outputs shifted to go ever so slightly more in these directions. He took his results to his employers at Boeing, concerned that if an REG could be affected, so might the sensitive instrumentation in the cockpit of an aircraft. They showed interest in his experiments, looking closely at his findings. Finally they concluded that the effect was just too small to present a real concern. They were probably right, and yet the deeper significance of Schmidt's findings was beginning to dawn on him. As subtle as these effects were, if they are real, then the implications overturn basic assumptions both about the mind, and perhaps the nature of reality itself.

SHIFTING PROBABILITIES

In 1976, physicist Robert Jahn was serving as Dean of Princeton University's School of Engineering and Applied Science. An expert in high temperature plasma dynamics, for many years he had directed a leading research program in advanced aerospace propulsion systems. The highly respected physicist, much loved by his students, had contributed to nearly three decades of NASA spaceflight missions. One afternoon, a young electrical engineering student approached him in his office. She had learned of Schmidt and his REG research and had become curious to see for herself if the mind-matter effect was real. Jahn was skeptical but concluded that the development of the REG itself would make for a good independent project for his student. To his surprise however, her pilot studies began producing interesting results. By the time she graduated, Jahn had carried out a number of his own experiments. Their apparent success intrigued him sufficiently that he decided to begin his own formal research into the phenomenon. He established a modest program in a small laboratory in an out-of-the-way corner of the engineering school, which became known as the 'PEAR,' laboratory - standing for Princeton Engineering Anomalies Research. In 1979, Brenda Dunne, a developmental psychologist from the University of Chicago, joined the program adopting the position of laboratory manager. In the following months the PEAR team grew to half a dozen interdisciplinary research staff consisting of psychologists, physicists and data analysts. The program would aim for an unprecedented empirical standard in psi research, hoping to determine once and for all if the mind-matter effect was real. After exploring various options for a new generation of REG, the researchers decided to use a microelectronic noise source. It would derive its 'coin-flip' process from a random flow of electrons as they either collide with, or pass through a barrier – a phenomenon known as 'quantum tunneling'. Like Schmidt's earlier REG, which had used the decay of radioactive material as a random source, the REG developed at PEAR would also be driven by quantum indeterminism: fundamentally probabilistic events that defy predictability. Outputs were recorded in trials consisting of 200 binary bits per second. Imagine flipping 200 coins at once. You could expect about 100 to land as 'heads' and 100 to land as 'tails.' Similarly with the REG, chance predicts that the average one-second trial should produce approximately 100 high counts and 100 low counts. Under normal conditions, when the REG is simply left to run, its total output quickly stabilizes to 50% high counts and 50% low. The standard experiment consisted of three runs with an equal number of trials. In one run, a participant would intend to produce more high counts; in another, more low counts; and in a third run, called a 'baseline,' no attempt would be made to influence the REG. The order of this three-stage process was randomized as a safeguard against any internal bias in the instrument. Regardless of their results all trials were diligently recorded; both automatically by a computer and by hand in a logbook. Participants in these experiments consisted largely of students and university visitors. They were asked simply to focus on the REG and intend to produce more high or low counts in accordance with the given trial's pre-assigned intention. Sure enough, the distributions were often seen to shift, ever so slightly, in the direction of their intention.[3] As the first months of research passed, the scientists watched as the overall results for the different trials began creeping away from each other. As experiments continued, these small deviations compounded, becoming highly statistically significant. When subject to the intending mind of a participant, order was somehow being introduced to the system, shifting the outputs to go either higher or lower. All participants were unpaid volunteers, making no claims to special abilities. Those that carried out many trials were also shown to have idiosyncratic styles, producing their own unique signatures in the data. Somehow the internal order of the directed mind was extending beyond the normally accepted limits of the body, introducing order into a physical system. The results hinted at the necessity of a radical new theory of human consciousness, in which mind is truly continuous with the world.

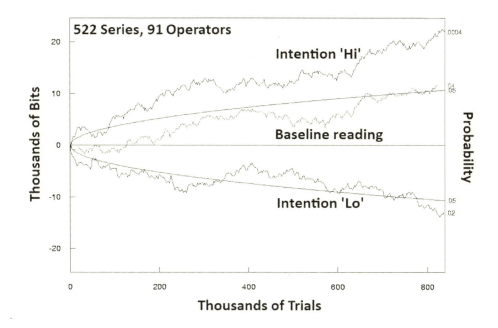

This graph displays the compiled data of more than 800,000 trials per intention. The pre-assigned intentions for high or low count runs were typically abbreviated to 'hi' and 'lo'. The trend of results in direction with pre-stated intentions is visible.[4]

One series of experiments was designed to run across great distances, yet the effect seemed mysteriously unbound by space. Even across thousands of miles, participants appeared able to shift the underlying order of the REG. During experiments the REG ran in an isolated room with no research personnel present. The laboratory staff would take turns initiating and recording the runs, which were also conducted 'blind', meaning they had no knowledge of what intention had been assigned until after the data was logged. Despite going to great lengths to avoid any possible problems with the experiments, in trials conducted over vast distances effects were observed that were eerily similar in magnitude to experiments conducted by participants within several feet of the REG.[5]

More recently, in 2014, large distance mind-matter effects were explored by an independent research team in Italy.[6] Led by psychologist Patrizio Tressoldi, the study took its inspiration from the mind-matter experiments at IONS discussed in the previous chapter. As we saw, the IONS researchers had found that individuals with attentional training – typically experience in some form of meditative practice, often produced more consistent effects. The Italian team considered that such individuals might also produce greater effects on REGs. Participants with an average of seven years meditative experience, located at EvenLab in Florence, were tasked with influencing an REG running some 190 kilometers away at the psychology department of Padua University. 102 experimental sessions were run with the same number of controls sessions in which the REG produced data without anyone attempting to influence it. The results were highly statistically significant. Within a predetermined cutoff period the REG exceeded a pre-stated deviation from chance in 82.3% of trials. During the control sessions however, the same deviation was recorded in only 13.7%. Their results offered further compelling evidence that aspects of the mind are uninhibited by space.

Jahn and his colleagues at PEAR had also made another surprising observation. They found that participants could achieve significant results regardless of whether sessions ran simultaneously with the REG, or if participants attempted to influence data that had already been produced.[7] Schmidt had also seen this bizarre, even paradoxical influence across time in his earlier experiments. He had set up an REG to run trials with their outcomes recorded onto magnetic tape. Without being observed by the experimenter or anyone else, the binary random data was calibrated into stereo audio clicks. At a later time a participant wearing headphones would listen to the clicks, playing into either the left or right ear. Schmidt asked his participants to attempt to influence the REG, this time intending to hear more clicks to the left or to the right side. Just as with experiments in which participants had attempted to influence the REG in real time, the distributions in these temporally displaced studies were also subtly shifted in line with the pre-defined intentions.[8] This retro causal influence, as we saw in the previous chapter, was later observed by the IONS researchers, when participants were shown to mysteriously influence photons as they had behaved in the past. We'll return to the mind's relationship to time in chapter 9, but perhaps the most profound implication of the mind-matter studies is that not only do they suggest that the mind is in some way tethered to reality at a deep level, but that this relationship is meaningfully related to psychological processes. Mental volitions and intentions appear to carry real currency in the underlying order of the physical world.

Nearly three decades after opening, by the time the PEAR laboratory closed its doors in 2007, the program had collected an enormous body of evidence that could not be reconciled within any conventional understanding of mind and consciousness. While the mind-matter evidence clearly defied classical physics, quantum physics pointed enigmatically to the role of conscious observers in the outcomes of experiments. The mind-matter experiments supported this radical but compelling interpretation, yet the rest of the scientific community was circumspect. PEAR's findings were met with suspicion and incredulity. In conventional knowledge these effects are simply impossible. While some scientists were intrigued, other's either ignored the program's findings altogether or simply dismissed them out of hand. Career skeptics and science communicators, incredulous of the radical implications, have confidently assumed critical errors must have been committed, either in their experimental designs, data collection techniques or statistical analyses. In point by point responses to published criticism however, PEAR's technical advisors have repeatedly argued that the experiments were well designed and that the reported effects are highly unlikely to be due to error.

Jahn and his colleagues had thought long and deeply about what their findings could mean. Their years of research led them to believe that for any hope of quantifying consciousness, a new 'science of the subjective' must be pursued. In their visioning of this new science, consciousness or awareness would be recognized as an intrinsic feature of reality – a kind of ordering principle, with an active, participatory role in the world. As we will now explore, other research has continued to support this view.

COLLECTIVE CONSCIOUSNESS

In the course of running experiments with the REG, another strange and unexpected effect was observed by the PEAR researchers. The REG seemed to ambiently respond to distinct shifts in the mental activity of laboratory personnel. Investigating further, they embarked on a series of experiments employing the REGs in a new way. These experiments became known as 'FieldREG'.[9] Using an REG connected to a portable laptop, the researchers attended a diverse range of public events, including group meditations, musical and theatrical performances, lectures and sports matches. During these experiments the REG ran continuously, with its unobserved output data recorded in a time-indexed file. Qualitative notes taken by the attending researcher marked moments when shifts in group attention appeared to occur. Such moments might occur during the climax of a theatrical performance, or when the home team scores in a football match. This time-indexed journal would later be compared to the data generated at the same time. Over many such events, the FieldREG experiments indeed produced positive findings. Moments of high emotion, suspense, or a shared experience of some kind were often found to correlate with statistically significant deviations from chance. Events that did not engage the attendees, on the other hand, such as administrative or business meetings, produced little or no such departures from statistical randomness. Positive results seemed to accompany groups participating in similar mental states. The effect, the researchers realized, while subtle in magnitude, was a real, repeatable phenomenon. Mental coherence among groups of individuals was somehow reflected in the underlying order of the physical world.

Psychologist Roger Nelson, a long-time member of the PEAR research staff, had become intrigued by the unorthodox ideas of 20th century French philosopher, Pierre Teilhard de Chardin. Teilhard had argued that, over billions of years, the natural course of evolution would lead life and consciousness to saturate the entire universe, culminating in a singularity of complexity and intelligence he called the *Omega Point*.[10] Long before this climactic feat, he predicted that the biospheres of entire worlds would become sufficiently integrated to constitute global planetary intelligences he called *Noospheres*, meaning 'mental spheres'. While Nelson was circumspect toward some of Teilhard's more spiritual ideas, he began wondering if human consciousness did indeed coalesce at global scales. Today's advances in technology mean that we live in an age of instant information – where people around the planet become captivated, shocked, moved, and inspired by the same world events. Since large groups of minds appeared to influence REGs, perhaps a coalescing of entire populations of minds would as well.

In 1997, during a conference in Germany, embryonic ideas were beginning to solidify. Nelson and Radin light-heartedly explored the possibility of a giant global electroencephalograph (an instrument used to detect electrical activity in the brain) consisting of a vast network of REGs. 'An Electro *Gaia* Gram' they mused. On reflection, Nelson realized this idea was not as outlandish as it might first seem. Indeed, a network of REGs could conceivably be installed all around the planet, with their outputs transmitted via the Internet to a central server. Perhaps significant world events would stir enough minds to create a detectable ripple in this ocean of minds. Would such a network be sensitive enough to detect it? It seemed equally possible that any such interaction would simply be too diffuse to be measured in this way. When small-scale pilot experiments produced intriguing results, however, Nelson was motivated to proceed. With the help of colleagues and independent researchers, he began building a global, continuously running network of REGs and in August 1998, the international collaboration now known as the 'Global Consciousness Project' or 'GCP' was launched. As interested researchers around the world volunteered to host an REG, soon a vast network stretched over some 40 countries.

In this ongoing study each REG collects 200 bits of information per second, with its data continuously transmitted to a central server. Here it is automatically added to a permanent archive. Together, this network of REGs contributes to a global picture of their relative coherence in any given moment. All of this data is presented transparently online, along with details of the researchers' standard methods of analysis. So, does the activity of this network actually correlate with events marshaling humanity's collective attention? The answer, it seems, is yes.

A random event generator used by the Global Consciousness Project known as *Orion*.

Before we look at some of the GCP's evidence, a few words about its epistemology. The GCP is primarily anthropocentric (human oriented). While most of us would probably attribute at least some consciousness to the rich biosphere of other life forms with which we share our planet, how these minds might affect the network remains difficult to predict and interpret for obvious reasons. The GCP is therefore primarily concerned with events of collective significance for human beings. Modern technology connects entire human populations in a global society such that when significant events unfold, it is almost impossible for us to remain unaware of them. Our modern technologies make us uniquely sensitive to events that carry collective meaning. The researchers established stringent criteria for categorizing and identifying global events, and as these kinds of scenarios unfolded over the following years, they indeed appear to correlate with increases of order in the network. To date events have included mass meditations, untimely deaths of public figures, natural disasters such as devastating earthquakes and tsunamis, major international sports events, New Year celebrations and terrorist attacks.[11]

In order to understand the significance of these often very subtle effects, we will briefly examine two particularly human-significant occasions from the GCP database. These are the moment of the new millennium and the devastating events of 9/11. If the network of REGs really does respond to dramatic shifts in attention within human populations, it is difficult to imagine two better candidates in recent history.

The greatly anticipated arrival of the third millennium not only promised to be the collective experience of the century, for many people, underlying narratives of social meaning attributed high significance to this event. Among many there was widespread concern that technological glitches produced by computer clocks moving into a new century would cause them to reset, producing catastrophic technical difficulties and computer crashes. Some feared planes might literally fall out of the sky. In some minds this date stirred fears of an apocalypse. Given all these factors, the turn of the new millennium promised to direct the collective attention and emotions of the human population toward a single, greatly anticipated moment. For this experiment, the REG network data was analyzed respective of its time zone, compiled so that the precise times of the millennium shift could be observed as a single, composite event. Sure enough, three seconds before midnight, as billions of minds anticipated the impending moment, the network sharply deviated from randomness. In an independent analysis, Radin calculated that odds of a shift of that scale, so close to midnight, could be associated with odds of 1,300 to 1. [12] At this globally significant and impending moment, some form of pervasive resonant mental peak in attention had occurred, which had apparently been recorded by the network. A second dramatic event was the unforeseen and world-changing terrorist attacks of September 11th 2001. As this shocking series of events unfolded and people all around the world looked on in horror, the GCP's network generated its data. Radin carried out an independent analysis. While there is no ordinary reason for why the behavior of separate REGs should synchronize, when he calculated the 'intercorrelation' value over the entire year of 2001, he found that the 9/11 data had produced the single largest value of *any day that year*.[13] For reasons yet to be understood, the dramatic changes in the network's behavior actually began just over four hours prior to the first plane hitting *Tower One*. Was this a collective sense of foreboding – a kind of mass subconscious precognition of events already set in motion to take place? Further analysis revealed that the network variance was also most highly concentrated over the east coast of the USA, the actual location of the terrorist attacks. But why should there be any localization of the effect if, as thought by many researchers, psi effects are non-local? Nelson considered that this might have been due to the generally heightened significance of these events to people in that area. Another possibility was that the network was responding to the sheer volume of attention being directed to that location. The events of 9/11 carried lasting sociological, cultural, and geopolitical implications that impacted the entire world. Even though analysis of unforeseen events such as these are necessarily retroactive, the events of 9/11 were of precisely the sort we could expect to have a large effect on the network, and the results apparently bore this out.

The GCP is, in an important sense, unique in psi research. The network itself was never the subject of the world's attention; indeed, the vast majority of people remain completely unaware of its existence. And yet their minds seemed to be affecting it. Even without any direct intention, the coherence of minds and the underlying order of matter appear to mysteriously reflect one another. As psi researcher Adam Curry has commented, 'We do have an unexplained impact on these devices, meaning that we do have an unexplained impact or influence on the world around us.'

BURNING MAN FESTIVAL

Researchers at IONS have also conducted REG experiments exploring collective mind-matter effects. An annual destination of recent years has been the eclectic environment of *Burning Man* festival. Every year, tens of thousands of people descend on the temporary city of Black Rock in the desert of northern Nevada. Attendees look forward to a week of music and Bohemian entertainments of all kinds. Each year, the central attraction is the highly anticipated 'burning of the man', in which a large wooden effigy is ignited on the central playa – an event accompanied with fireworks, music, and colorful visual displays. In their report documenting experiments carried out over the 2012 event, the IONS researchers outlined their starting assumptions.

'The underlying hypothesis in studies of this type, dubbed 'field consciousness' experiments, is that mind and matter are complementary aspects of a more fundamental, holistic reality. As an analogy, the idea is that subjective mind and objective matter may be like heads and tails on a coin. These two aspects of nature may appear to be quite different from one another when examined separately, but from a broader perspective they may be seen as part of an intimate relationship by virtue of being connected to, or part of, the same 'substance.' [15]

The researchers predicted that an REG running on the central playa for the duration of the festival would display the highest departure from ordinary random behavior when collective attention was at its highest intensity – a time they believed would coincide with the initiation of the burning of the man ceremony. In keeping with the artistic spirit of the festival, the output of their REG was set up to animate a laser that grew brighter and slower in response to departures in the REG's ordinary random behavior. A second hypothesis was that the larger network of the Global Consciousness Project would also record statistically significant departures during the same time, though perhaps to a lesser degree. Their third hypothesis was that a second major event on the Sunday night, known as the 'temple burn' would also be associated with a significant increase in statistical order in the REGs. All three of these predictions proved to be accurate. Analysis of the data collected during the burning of the man ceremony was associated with modest odds against chance of

250 to 1. This result, as the researchers discussed in their report, could be anticipated to occur by chance about 4 times if the same experiment were carried out each year for a millennium. But even in the unlikely event that they had simply 'gotten lucky', the combined statistical likelihood of the three experiments was associated with odds against chance of 106,420 to 1. [16]

Flames engulf a wooden effigy during the 'Burning of the Man' ceremony.

During the festival, the president of IONS, Dr. Cassandra Vieten gave a public presentation, calling for open-mindedness toward this unconventional area of study. She pointed to the example of how the scientific establishment eventually came round to the existence of electromagnetism, noting that it wasn't until after Michael Faraday's death that his discovery was accepted by the skeptical scientific community of his day. Similarly, the existence of germs, the discovery of which has saved countless lives, took over a century to gain acceptance. The science of these so-called 'collective consciousness' effects, argued Vieten, could carry extraordinary and as yet unrealized implications. Vocal applause met the end of her talk, which she concluded by saying,

> 'Let us not hold scientific investigation back by the limits of our current imagination.'[17]

Following the apparent success of their experiments, IONS researchers returned to Burning Man the following year with designs on a further study. This time instead of one REG, *six* were installed around the central playa. They were of several types, sampling their random processes from different sources. Three REGs derived their data from standard electron tunneling. Two of which were the familiar *Orion* model used by the GCP – and another, the *REG-1* produced by *Psyleron*. Two REGs derived their data from the decay of a weakly radioactive material, in a design similar to the REG first developed by Helmut Schmidt. The final REG, of Swiss design, was the *Quantis,* a model sampling the random behavior of photons as they are either reflected by, or pass through, a half silvered mirror. All the REGs were developed to be resistant to the potential influence of electromagnetic and ionizing radiation, vibrations, changes in temperature and electrical surges.

As 9 pm approached on the evening of the 31st of August 2013, the attention of some 65,000 festival attendees was drawn toward a large wooden statue in anticipation of a sign that the ceremony had begun. With the local network of

REGs running silently in the background, a few seconds after 9pm, excitement rippled through the crowd as the arms of the effigy began rising into the air. The cross-correlation between the REGs spiked suddenly, producing a highly statistically significant result. Festival attendees would have to wait some 30 minutes before flames were visible, yet precisely when collective attention was anticipated to be at its highest, the network of REGs dramatically departed from their ordinary random behavior.[18]

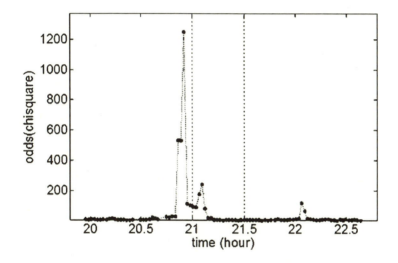

This graph shows the 6 REGs' departure from randomness between 8 and just after 10:30pm. The data is presented as odds against chance. The perforated line to the left marks the beginning of the ceremony, moments before which, a large spike appears in the data.[19]

This moment of collective anticipation, experienced by many minds at once, seemed to have produced an increase of order in these usually random systems. 'The nice thing about this effect', commented Radin, who had led the study, 'is that it is more or less repeatable. You get an event that's big enough, and enough people paying attention, you see changes in entropy.'[20] Indeed, compelling results were also obtained the following year.[21]

With the REGs in place for the 2014 Burning Man ceremony, disaster struck when the researchers discovered that the REG's memory storage had been installed incorrectly, leading to no usable data being recorded. Whilst the researchers were disappointed, all was not lost. The researchers set their sights on the temple burn ceremony taking place the following night. After ensuring the same issue would not be repeated, the researchers arranged ten REGs in proximity of the event. The temple burn is known for having a very different vibe to the burning man ceremony. Thousands of people affix their written prayers and wishes onto an elaborate wooden structure before it is ceremoniously ignited. Sure enough, the experiment produced highly statistically significant results. Just prior to the event, with crowds gathered, the REGs began behaving more like each other than anticipated by chance. This coherence sustained for the duration of the ceremony, following which the ten REGs reassumed their ordinary random behavior.[22]

Do these findings really indicate that the collective attention of thousands of minds is reflected in the underlying order of the physical world? Researchers continue to support this extraordinary interpretation, but are we ready to accept it? All these findings are, of course, controversial and when not completely ignored, are often subject to heated skeptical criticism by the mainstream scientific community. However, from the moment researchers acknowledged that consciousness was even a real phenomenon, occupying a real place in nature – if even just in our skulls, they had unmistakably left behind the academic consensus. Over the years the Global Consciousness Project and the independent research it inspired has continued to generate compelling evidence that mind and world reflect each other in ways modern science is yet to grasp. Still to be understood is how these microphysical effects may compound to produce larger effects in the world. Is this intuitive arrow of causation even correct? While these questions continue to pose difficult challenges, the results unmistakably indicate that, in a still mysterious manner, mind and matter reflect one another. These experiments also suggest that minds have the capacity to coalesce in meaningful ways – that our minds may not be as separate from each other as we tend to imagine. In the next chapter we encounter further evidence of this arriving from clinical experiments exploring *telepathy*.

'These disturbing phenomena seem to deny all our usual scientific ideas. How we should like to discredit them! Unfortunately the statistical evidence, at least for telepathy, is overwhelming.' [23]

Alan Turing
Father of modern computer science

6. ENTANGLED PERCEPTIONS

In the 1960's, psychologist Charles Tart performed a series of experiments, the findings of which were so surprising, they briefly captured wide spread attention. Many successful replications followed, which have continued to the present day. Measuring the brain activity of emotionally bonded participants using an electroencephalograph (EEG), Tart found that an isolated person's brain activity could entrain with that of another person who was spatially separated from them and responding to a randomized stimulus.[1] The original study, published in the *International Journal of Parapsychology* in 1963, was followed two years later by a similar experiment carried out by T.D Duane and Thomas Behrendt, with identical twins. Their study was published in the respected scientific journal, *Science*.[2] The researchers found that when one twin was instructed to close their eyes – an act that naturally increases alpha rhythm levels in the brain – these rhythms also increased in the other twin who was in a separate room. These two studies suggested that the mental activities associated with the brain were not limited to a given individual, and that psychologically bonded people could become psychically entrained.

Do twins share a deeper connection?

Publicity of these extraordinary assertions led several independent research teams to attempt to replicate the effect. Out of ten studies initially conducted, eight reported statistically significant results. One of these studies was published in the mainstream journal, *Nature*.[3] Just as in earlier experiments, correlations were found in the brain activities of separated participants. Typically in these experiments, one participant, known as the 'sender', is exposed to a stimulus such as a randomized flashing light, which produces distinct observable peaks in brain activity. Meanwhile another participant, known as the 'receiver,' is situated a distance away in a dimly lit electromagnetically shielded room. This participant is also connected to brain activity monitoring instrumentation. Despite having no possible knowledge of the flashes exposed to the sender, the receiver's brain activity has been found to correlate with the flashes shown to their partner, with discrete though significant increases in their brain activity during these times.

The existence of this correlation confounds our ordinary assumptions about the mind's isolation from the physical world. Furthermore, shielding protocols have ruled out explanation by electromagnetic signals somehow emanating from the body. The effect, like that of the mind-matter experiments, seems appropriately defined as 'nonlocal'. In 2003, after performing their own successful replications of this strange effect, electroencephalography specialist Jiří Wackermann and his colleagues concluded by saying,

> 'We are facing a phenomena which is neither easy to dismiss as a methodological failure or a technical artifact nor understood as to its nature. No biophysical mechanism is presently known that could be responsible for the observed correlations between EEGs of two separate subjects.'[4]

In 2004, a research team at Bastyr University led by physician Leanna Standish reported successful results of yet another study.[5] The researchers had tested 30 pairs of individuals from a population specially selected to share strong emotional bonds. These were typically romantic couples, siblings or family members. Upon testing these couples, the researchers identified a single pair that produced the highest regularity of an effect. The study itself focused exclusively on them. In the Bastyr study, instead of using EEG instruments, the receiver participant was lying down inside a functional magnetic resonance imaging (fMRI) scanner – an instrument used to measure blood flow to specific regions of the brain. The sender participant, again located in a distant room, was exposed to a randomized flashing display. Just as previous studies had found, during these periods, significant increases in blood flow were recorded in the receiver's brain. Moreover, the results indicated that these increases of blood-flow occurred in the appropriate area of the brain to be associated with a response to an optical stimulus: the *visual cortex*. Though the participant reported no direct awareness of it, their cortical activity correlated with the other individual's experience. The specially selected couple produced a highly significant overall effect, with odds against chance of 14,000 to 1.

The same year, researchers at IONS reported the results of another successful study using and EEG.[6] Pairs of participants had decided amongst themselves who would act as sender or receiver. The receiver was then isolated in an electromagnetically and acoustically shielded chamber. The sender was located in a dimly lit room approximately 30 feet away. In this study the stimulus was a live video image of the receiver's face, appearing on a screen via closed-circuit television. During the experimental period, the receiver's face would appear at random times to the sender. Like the flashing displays used in previous experiments, this sudden appearance of the receiver's face would naturally cause a distinct increase of activity in the sender's brain. It was also anticipated to serve as a reinforcement of the psychological connection between the participants. The results of this study were also statistically significant, with a probability that the observed correlations were due to chance calculated at 5,000 to 1.

These controversial experiments support the view that some aspect of our mental activity extends beyond our brains, to coalesce with the minds of others. They suggest that when we meaningfully connect with other people in our lives, deeper relationships are being cultivated than we might realize. These relationships, like other apparent examples of psi phenomena, also appear to be nonlocal – uninhibited by the normal constraints of space and time. When we feel a profound bond with others, might we literally be perceiving our deeper shared identity? An underlying interconnectivity between organisms would provide clear advantages for survival and, in explicit ways, may have been evolutionarily selected for. Sensing the attention of a dangerous animal crouched in the grasses, a mother's instinct that her child needs her, sensing when a distant member of the tribe is in danger – critical moments such as these may have engendered the evolution of subtle psychic senses.

Psi experiments are often motivated by reports of 'everyday' psi experiences in the lives of ordinary people. How often have we thought about someone just before our phone rings and that same person is calling? There's no doubt that many everyday experiences appearing to be psychic are better explained by more mundane explanations. But if there's a grain of truth to any of these experiences, it ought to be possible to measure them in the laboratory. We now turn to extraordinary research exploring the possibility that thoughts and ideas can be mysteriously shared between minds outside of the known senses.

7. SHARING INNER SPACE

In the early 1970s, psi researchers became interested in exploring the possibility of subtle extrasensory information, normally lost amid the 'noise' of the ordinary waking mind. They considered that these subtle psychic impressions, if they existed, might be detected more easily under conditions of sensory deprivation. They had good reason to suspect that altered states would be conducive to observing psi effects. Meditation, the influence of psychoactive drugs, dreaming, and the verge of sleep are all states long associated with anecdotes of 'everyday' psi experiences. In this time, psi researchers turned their attention to a type of sensory deprivation state known as the 'ganzfeld.' Meaning 'entire field' in German, the method was first developed in the 1930's by gestalt psychologist Wolfgang Metzger as a tool to explore visual perception. In the ganzfeld a participant sits comfortably in a reclined chair, wearing semi translucent eye shields permitting through only a diffused red light. This is combined with headphones playing a continuous soft, white noise; somewhat reminiscent of the sound of sea waves crashing in the distance. After a few minutes relaxing in this featureless sensory field, the participant enters into a hypnogogic state, somewhere between waking and dreaming. As the mind searches for sensory information, they experience an amplification of subconscious impressions, producing mild visual and auditory 'hallucinations'. Researchers would now employ this condition as a possible psi-conducive state in a new type of telepathy experiment. The findings of these ganzfeld studies have continued to the present day, and are considered by many psi researchers to have produced some of the most compelling evidence of psi ever collected under laboratory conditions. So what happens in a ganzfeld experiment?

ENTER THE GANZFELD

These experiments would follow a design similar to dream telepathy studies, first pioneered by psychologist Stanley Krippner in the 1960s.[1] In the new Ganzfeld experiments, with the participant no longer needing to be asleep, data could be generated much more quickly. A prototypical ganzfeld experiment involves two participants, one acting as the receiver and one as the sender. At the beginning of the experiment, the 'receiver' is taken to an isolated ganzfeld chamber that has been acoustically and electromagnetically shielded. Seating herself in a reclined chair, the receiver places on the headphones and eye shields and begins relaxing into the featureless sensory field. After a few minutes the dreamlike state characteristic of the ganzfeld sets in. Meanwhile, the other participant, the 'sender' is taken to another isolated area at least 50 feet away. Here they are presented with an image or short film clip, selected at random from a set of four possible targets – as categorically different from each other as possible. This set of four targets has itself been randomly chosen from a larger archive of target sets. For the next 30 minutes the sender's task is to attempt to mentally project this target to the receiver. While this is happening, the receiver is encouraged to speak aloud any images or impressions that come to mind. In some versions of the experiment, the sender can hear the receiver's impressions as they verbalize them via a one-way audio system. This acts as a form of feedback for the sender, who may choose to refine or alter their mental sending strategy in response. After the allotted time, the receiver is asked to remove the headphones and eye shields and remain in the chamber, awaiting the final stage of the experiment.

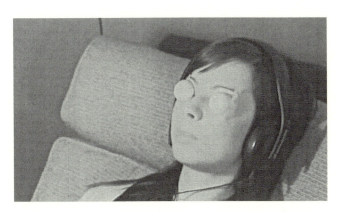

A student takes part in a ganzfeld study.

Before being asked to identify the image or clip she felt was being sent, the receiver listens back to her verbal impressions recorded during the session. The experimenter then presents her with a set of four images or clips, one of which is the target. She ranks them 1 to 4 with number one being the image or clip that best matched her impressions. Only then is the sender participant permitted to leave the isolated sending location and share the actual target with the experimenter and receiver. Only if the correct image is ranked first is the session counted as a 'hit'.

As in the earlier dream telepathy studies, the researcher conducting the experiment is 'blinded' from knowing the target, meaning they have no knowledge of what the target for the session has been until the experiment is finished. This ensures that the experimenter cannot inadvertently provide any subtle cues to the receiver during the judging process. Typically ganzfeld experiments have 4 possible targets. This gives a 1-in-4 likelihood that a hit will be achieved by chance. If nothing but random chance is at play, participants should guess correctly 25% of the time. Intriguingly, when inclusive meta-analyses are conducted on many studies, hit rates approach approximately 32%.[2] Given the high number of studies, this result far exceeds what can reasonably be anticipated by chance.

In 1982, Charles Honorton presented a paper summarizing the results of all published ganzfeld experiments reported to that time. The high statistical significance supporting what Honorton referred to as 'anomalous information transfer' was so surprising to skeptic Ray Hyman, that he was at first convinced that Honorton had made a critical error in his calculations. He decided to perform his own meta-analysis to be published alongside Honorton's. Of the 34 studies published to that time, both scientists jointly decided to include those 28 studies designed to predict a 25% hit-rate by chance. Of these 28 studies, 23 had been statistically significant, and when completed, their joint analysis showed that odds of the results occurring by chance were greater than a billion to one.[3] Though he remained unconvinced of the existence of telepathy, Hyman agreed that these results could not be attributed to chance. Something else was going on.

Following his joint publication with Hyman, Honorton dedicated his work to improving the ganzfeld experimental design. In new experiments he used computers to automate every stage of the experiment. Over the next seven years he conducted an additional 354 trials using this 'auto-ganzfeld' technique. The combined results of these subsequent experiments were comparable with those of the previous meta-analyses: a 35% hit rate overall.[4] Commenting on Honorton's later findings, the still-skeptical Hyman conceded,

> 'Honorton's experiments have produced intriguing results. If independent laboratories can produce similar results with the same relationships and with the same attention to rigorous methodology, then parapsychology may indeed have finally captured its elusive quarry.'[5]

Hyman, a committed skeptic, was never swayed by the research that followed, yet many researchers are convinced that later studies have indeed continued to produce psi effects. In 2004, Dean Radin conducted an in-depth meta-analysis of all reported ganzfeld studies between 1974 to that time.[6] Across 88 studies the average hit rate was approximately 32% – a full 7% greater than anticipated by chance. He calculated that the likelihood of this result, over this many sessions, could be associated with odds against chance of one in *29 quintillion*. As well as the rigorously tight controls used in these experiments, researchers had gone to unprecedented lengths in response to skeptical criticism. They invited professional magicians to overlook experimental protocols, used industrial horns to test for possible audio leakages in the soundproof chamber, and painstakingly examined entire target archives in search of possible fingerprint smudges.

As is the standard in the social and medical sciences, researchers also have to be aware of the possibility that there exist numerous unreported, perhaps unsuccessful studies conducted in the same area – the so-called 'file drawer effect.' Perhaps studies producing null results were considered uninteresting by researchers and subsequently were left unpublished. If enough unpublished studies exist, there is the worrying possibility that the failure to report them inflates the appearance of positive results. Skeptics have frequently pointed to this explanation when dismissing the ganzfeld telepathy evidence. However, standard statistical methods can be used to address this possible confound. One such method involves calculating the number of studies with null results required to account for the overall effect size as a chance outcome. When Radin conducted this analysis on the ganzfeld literature it quickly became transparent that selective publishing could not explain the results. He calculated that more than two thousand unreported full studies with results at chance, each with an average of 36 trials, would be required to explain these findings by selective publishing. His analysis was described in his 2006 book, *Entangled Minds*, where he concluded,

> 'To generate this many sessions would mean continually running ganzfeld sessions 24 hours a day, 7 days a week, for 36 years, and for not one of those sessions to see the light of day. That's not plausible.' [7]

In 2005, two skeptical psychologists published a paper in an effort to put to rights what they considered to be the 'flawed research literature' on telepathy.[8] They observed that existing studies indeed seemed to point to the existence of telepathy. This was a problem for the skeptical scientists. Convinced that fowl play was afoot, they decided to conduct their own Ganzfeld experiments. The surprise came when, after analyzing eight of their own studies, they found statistically significant results. Furthermore, the average hit rate was approximately 32% – dangerously similar to that reported in other meta-analyses. These findings, the researchers acknowledged were, '...precariously close to demonstrating humans do have psychic powers.'[9] Of course, this wasn't enough to convince the scientists that a psi effect had been observed. In an effort to mitigate these potentially embarrassing results, they decided that a further previously unplanned study was necessary. Going out on a limb, they abandoned the Ganzfeld literature, proposing a previously untested hypothesis they called 'psychic theory', which they summarized as follows,

> 'In the ganzfeld procedure, participants are run in pairs. According to psychic theory, if one member of the pair is psychic (P) but the other is not (n) there will be no transmission of information. Only PP pairs can successfully send and receive messages.'[10]

When these experiments produced statistically significant *negative* scores, the researchers were vindicated. Ignoring all the existing studies and even their own data, this single final study, looking at an untested hypothesis, led them to conclude,

> 'Due to this last data set, we do not believe that humans possess telepathic powers.'[11]

Perhaps unsurprisingly, their conclusions have not been convincing to other researchers. Over the years, dialogue between researchers and skeptics have seen the ganzfeld experiment continue to evolve. Modern studies are fully automated, eliminating any risk of experimenter error. These experiments may be about as close to a 'perfect' design as is likely to be achieved. A meta-analysis, published in *Psychological Bulletin* in 2010, included all computer-automated ganzfeld studies conducted between 1997 and 2008.[12] Authors Lance Storm, Patrizio Tressoldi, and Lorenzo Di Risio found an average hit rate of 32.2%. This may seem like a small effect, yet with this many studies, the odds of this result being due to chance is many trillions to one. The scientists also reported that psychological factors such as extraversion and belief in psi – previously observed to be predictive of psi receptivity in other experiments, were also visible in the ganzfeld studies.

So how does information in one person's mind get into someone else's? It's far from clear how these effects take place and many researchers remain agnostic toward possible theories. Given its apparently nonlocal nature, Radin has proposed that the effect is analogous to that of quantum entanglement.[13] No information is classically transferred between entangled particles; instead their states are *correlated*. He suggests that apparent instances of telepathy might occur in a similar way. Instead of some signal transmitting information between brains, the participants' minds may be entering into complimentary states, allowing shared experiences to occur. As Radin expressed in a correspondence with me, 'Quantum mechanics reminds us that the universe is ultimately a holistic, tightly integrated web, and thus it is not out of the question that no signals need pass between brains, and nothing needs to come into being. From a holistic perspective all brains are already connected to everything else from the get-go, and not just through space. Through time too.'[14] If we indeed live within such a holistic fabric, psi effects like telepathy might not only be permitted, but *anticipated*.

The development of brain interfacing technologies may one day permit reliable brain-to-brain communication. Indeed, there are already studies suggesting that this kind of pseudo-telepathy is possible. However, the psi telepathy evidence apparently hints toward a much deeper and profound connection between minds. So what does it *mean* if telepathy really happens? These 'communications anomalies' as researchers have termed them, raise a number of provocative questions. To what extent do our inner mental landscapes passively interpenetrate during everyday life? To what degree might we be always subtly exchanging information with others and our environments? People often speak of individuals as having 'vibes' or sharing their moods. The evidence suggests that there may be more happening here than ordinary sensory cues. Telepathy, if it is real, encourages us to take greater responsibility for our inner mental life, serving as a vivid reminder that we are each the owner of a mind that is only ever superficially separate from that of others. If consciousness reflects an intrinsic aspect of all reality, it invites us to consider ourselves, in an imminent sense, as part of a single, evolving experiential system. But if the mind is not bound by the classical constraints of space, what might be its relationship to *time*?

'People like us, who believe in physics, know that the distinction between past, present, and future is only a stubbornly persistent illusion.' [21]

Albert Einstein

8. MIND IN TIME

The possibility that mind may have aspects extending beyond the present has been explored through an extensive range of psi experiments. Known generally as *precognition*, it has been widely investigated throughout the last century. Results suggest that the mind is mysteriously spread out in time. In an early meta-analysis of all forced-choice precognition studies published between 1935 and 1987, Charles Honorton and Diane Ferrari concluded that participants typically score better at predicting a future stimulus than can reasonably be attributed to chance.[1] In their analysis of the literature they explored and ultimately rejected the explanation that design flaws were the cause of these apparent effects. Another observation born out of the data was that the act of participants receiving feedback seemed to play a significant role in observing psi. In recent years, precognition researchers have become increasingly interested in the role of the subconscious mind. Dean Radin, who has contributed extensively to the field of psi research, has also made important contributions to the study of precognition. In 1996, he published a series of experiments investigating the possibility that living beings have an innate though subconscious sense of their own future.[2] He predicted that if precognition was real, it might be visible in the physiological activity of the body just prior to the presentation of a stimulus. These first experiments focused on electrodermal activity (EDA) – tiny variations in the conductivity of the skin. EDA readings are often used in psychological studies to track emotional arousal. Radin decided to use this classic measure to explore the existence of subconscious precognition in the body.

In this experiment a participant sits in front of a blank monitor screen. Electrodes are placed on the index and middle fingers of their non-dominant hand. When ready, the participant clicks the mouse. This initiates a five second waiting period following which the computer randomly selects either a 'calm' or 'emotional' image, which then appears on the screen. Calm images consist of relaxing landscapes and mundane objects like furniture while emotional images consist of violent or erotic themes. Upon being selected by the computer the image is visible for 3 seconds. Participants are required to do no more than attend to the image. The screen then goes blank and a 10 second 'cool-down' period ensues. The cycle begins again when the computer prompts the participant to click the mouse and initiate another trial. This whole cycle repeats 40 times, taking approximately half an hour to complete.

Twenty-four people participated in Radin's first study. When he analyzed the data, their physiological activity indeed seemed to correlate with their future experience. Without being aware of it, participants' skin conductance was slightly more elevated during the 5-second period prior to experiencing emotional images. The odds of the results occurring by chance were approximately 1 in 500. He used standard analytical tools and data partitioning to distinguish between a possible psi effect and any ordinary anticipatory effects that might occur, such as during a series of calm images where the participant anticipates an emotional image is on its way. Any possible biases in the image randomization process that could provide subtle cues to the participant were considered and ruled out. After exploring and finally rejecting a range of other possible explanations, Radin eventually concluded that this might be a genuine psi effect. He called this unconscious form of precognition *presentiment*.

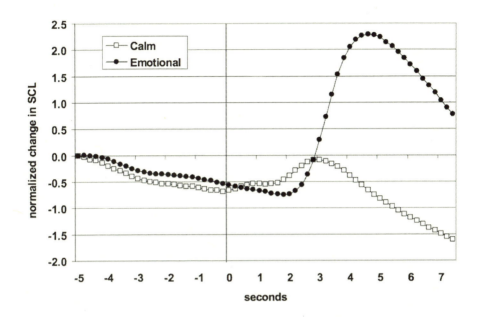

This graph displays cumulative trials of Radin's first presentiment experiment, involving 24 participants. SCL stands for 'skin conductance level.' The intersecting vertical line marks the point in time when the image is randomly selected and presented to the participant. Before this time, however, participants' skin conductivity can already be seen to have separated in line with their future experience.[3]

When Radin published in 1997, his findings were met with surprise and intrigue by his colleagues. The ensuing interest led to a series of replications. In later experiments presentiment effects were also identified in other physiological measures, including heart rate, blood flow and later in pupil dilation. Soon after hearing about Radin's study, first-skeptical physicist Dick Bierman responded by conducting a series of experiments with a near-identical design. His study was also successful. Surprised, he considered that if the effect was real, it should have inadvertently been measured in other mainstream studies where skin conductivity had been a variable. Bierman found three potential studies. One looked at the rate at which fear arises in animal-phobic participants, another investigated anticipatory responses in a gambling task, and a third explored the effect of emotional priming prior to the evaluation of Japanese characters. Re-analyzing the data of these studies, Bierman uncovered statistically significant evidence of a presentiment effect.[4]

Further evidence was obtained in 2002, when Bierman collaborated with psychologist Steven Scholte to explore the possibility of presentiment in the brain.[5] This time, functional magnetic resonance imaging (fMRI) was used to detect increases in blood flow in the brain just prior to the presentation of a stimulus. In this study both erotic and violent images were dispersed in a pool of calm images. While no overall significant effect was seen prior to violent imagery, a modest effect was recorded before presentation of erotic images with odds against chance of 320 to 1. The researchers also reported differing effects between genders, finding that while presentiment was observed in both females and males prior to the presentation of erotic imagery, only women had demonstrated a statistically significant effect prior to violent images. In 2003, neuroscientist James Spottiswoode and physicist Edwin May reported the findings of a successful study using sound as a stimulus.[6] Here, higher levels of EDA were measured just prior to a loud, randomly initiated tone. Their study, consisting of 125 participants, produced results associated with odds against chance of 1,250 to 1. In 2004, Rollin McCraty and his colleagues at the *Institute of Heart Math* published a study reporting anticipatory changes in heart rate just prior to an emotional stimulus.[7] To growing public interest, in 2008, Radin's classic presentiment experiment was successfully demonstrated in front of the cameras of the popular BBC science program, *Horizon*. Two years later he and three colleagues published a further study, this time exploring the possibility that the attentional capacities enhanced by meditative practices might make experienced practitioners predisposed to larger presentiment effects.[8] In meditation, experiences of timelessness are commonplace and often much more time passes during meditation than is subjectively perceived. The researchers wondered whether such experiences of timelessness reflect an aspect of awareness that extends beyond the present moment. They used EEG instrumentation to detect brain activity prior to and following the presentation of a randomized stimulus. Exploring two types of stimulus, an audio tone and a light flash, these experiments were also successful, suggesting that meditators indeed had a greater prevalence for presentiment than non-meditators.

REFLECTIONS OF THE FUTURE

In March 2011, social psychologist Daryl Bem published a paper in the *Journal of Personality and Social Psychology*, setting off a new wave of controversy in the academic community.[9] Bem's paper, 'Feeling the Future' was the culmination of eight years of research. This controversial paper by a highly respected academic apparently supported the unorthodox view that aspects of the human mind somehow extend across time. After analyzing virtually every detail of his study, a skeptical panel agreed that his methodology had been sound and cautiously recommended publication. His study consisted of nine experiments involving over a thousand participants. He hypothesized that if precognition really occurs it ought to be visible in ordinary psychological effects when they are 'time-reversed.' For example, in one experiment he showed participants a long list of words. A short time later they he asked them to recall as many of these words as possible. Shortly after finishing this task participants were presented a shorter list of words that had been randomly selected from the first list. Participant then typed these words out. Bem found that participants proved better at recalling words they would later be asked to type, even though they had no ordinary way of knowing what these words would be. In another of Bem's experiments he explored the well-known 'priming effect'. The priming effect can be demonstrated by showing someone an emotionally affective word like 'ugly' prior to being shown, say, a picture of some kittens. The brief cognitive dissonance between word and image predictably slows our ability to acknowledge that the picture was from a 'pleasant' or 'unpleasant' image category. In his experiments reversing this process however, Bem discovered that the same subtle interference was also found in trials where the word was presented *after* the image. The classic priming effect, well established in the psychological literature, also appeared to work in reverse.

Eight of Bem's nine experiments yielded small but statistically significant evidence of a psi effect.[10] The combined results of his study were associated with odds against chance at greater than a *billion to 1*. When this high profile study, by a respected social psychologist was published, the skeptical community took up arms. Even prior to its publication editorials were issued featuring health warnings urging caution and suspicion toward the heretical study. By March the following year, skeptical psychologist Chris French submitted an article to *The Guardian*, documenting his and two other skeptical scientists' failure to replicate Bem's findings.[11] Bem would later observe, however, that French did not mention anywhere in his article the two already existing successful replications prior to that time, nor the large body of successful preceding research that justified the initial study. Bem also observed that French presented his own, Richard Wiseman, and Stuart Ritchie's findings as three separate unsuccessful studies while in fact their total number of trials had been equivalent to just one.

In 2012 a meta-analysis of all presentiment studies conducted between 1978 and 2010 was published.[12] The authors Julia Mossbridge, Patrizio Tressoldi and Jessica Utts observed that overall the experimental quality had been high. Overall the studies supported the existence of a small but highly statistically significant effect. They also observed that studies using differing analytical controls to counter expectation bias did not produce varying effects. In 2014, a further review of the presentiment literature was published in *Frontiers in Human Neuroscience*. The authors concluded that people indeed seemed to unconsciously sense future events.[13] In their discussion the authors considered the possibility that quantum processes may function within the body's physiology and that these may reflect fundamental time symmetries inherent in physics. Another meta-analysis published later that same year featured several studies attempting to replicate Bem's experiments. The report included 90 studies overall, conducted across 30 laboratories in 13 countries.[14] The authors reported the existence of an effect to within a confidence of greater than 6 sigma – *several billion to one*. This, Radin later noted, is a statistical confidence greater than that which won the Nobel Prize in physics following the apparent discovery of the *Higgs Boson* particle in 2012. If the extraordinary claim of precognition requires extraordinary evidence, this it would seem, is it.

The existence of precognition may provide alternative explanations for well-established psychological effects. An example is the *Color Phi phenomenon*. Observing this effect involves presenting a participant or audience with two images typically shown in quick succession. The two images depict two different colored dots on different sides of a blank square. When shown quickly one after another, the first dot appears to move to become the second dot, changing color part way. Interestingly, the color of the second dot is routinely perceived prior to its presentation. In order to explain this effect from within the traditional paradigm of perception it is necessary to invoke a complex reverse referencing of perceptual processes known as 'postdiction.' Essentially, the brain tricks itself into thinking it had a later experience before an earlier one. The only alternative, as the philosopher Daniel Dennett has pointed out, is that the experience is *precognitive*.

> 'Unless there is precognition in the brain, the illusory content cannot be created until after some identification of the second spot occurs...'[15]

Dennett however, who is committed to a reductive view of consciousness, rejects all psi evidence out of hand and thus doesn't consider precognition to be a sensible explanation. The evidence, as we've seen, challenges this stance. As Radin and his colleagues have pointed out, the concept of time-symmetry is central to many of the fundamental equations of both classical and quantum physics. For presentiment to be possible the brain need only follow known principles in physics.[16]

Precognition seems, at least for the most part, to occur unconsciously to the individual. Psychologists have known since the time of Freud that many behaviors and desires have unconscious causes. The unconscious mind is capable of processing and responding to events we never knew we were aware of. Since the 1960s researchers have explored altered states of consciousness as a means to test the possibility that psi typically occurs in those normally hidden aspects of the human psyche. If psi is usually unconscious, it raises the question of its role in our daily lives. Psychologist David Luke suggested that psi in ordinary life may look more like luck. In a questionnaire carried out before a precognitive task, Luke and his colleagues gave a series of questions to participants relating to their 'perceived personal luckiness.' The study revealed that people's beliefs about luck positively correlated with psi performance.[17] Furthermore, as observed in other studies in the psi literature, openness to the possibility of psi was also an indicator of success in precognitive tasks. Luke's findings suggested that people's beliefs about psi are probably informed by their own experiences in everyday life. The effect isn't big enough to take on the house at the casino, but it's there, posing an unsettling challenge to mainstream assumptions about the mind.

Precognition appears to give rise to an unsettling paradox. It challenges our basic and deep-felt intuitions about causality. For example, if we make an alteration in response to a perceived future event, and this action results in that event not occurring, from where, we might ask, did this information arrive? Precognition continues to mystify all those that attempt to understand it. The deep challenges it poses are the reason precognition is among the most controversial of psi effects. Yet, just as we have needed to become comfortable with a strange and unintuitive physics, precognition may require us to rethink basic assumptions about perception. As Helmut Schmidt once wrote,

> '...[Precognition] seemed quite contrary to common sense. People asked by what 'mechanism' the outcome of a future random event could cause something (the subject's correct response) to occur in the present. But in spite of this conceptual difficulty, precognition continues to exist, and rather than wondering what is wrong with precognition, we should ask what is wrong with our common sense.'[18]

9. THE VIEW FROM HERE

There exists much psi research worthy of attention that falls beyond the scope of my brief survey of the evidence. For example, there is a compelling body of literature classed as 'direct mental interactions with living systems' known by the acronym 'DMILS'. Research of this type includes a body of studies that apparently show people can be subconsciously aware of when they are the subject of another person's attention. This effect has been explored both in studies where participants guess above chance in forced-choice experiments,[1] and when physiological activity such as skin conductance is compared between times another person's attention is trained on or away from them.[2] Pioneered by psychologist William Braud, anthropologist Marilyn Schlitz, and biologist Rupert Sheldrake, these studies apparently provide supportive empirical evidence of the much anecdotally reported 'sense of being stared at.'[3] In other DMILS studies, directed intention was apparently shown to subtly influence physiological processes in other forms of life, ranging from cells to mammals and fish.[4] Other studies reported similar anomalous relationships between humans. In a series of experiments carried out by Braud and Schlitz, participants were reported to reduce the electrodermal activity in another person simply by mentally intending to calm them.[5] In these experiments participants were in different rooms, with receiving subjects having no ordinary way of knowing if a given period had been designated as an experimental session or not. These studies apparently demonstrate that the ordering influence of conscious attention, well documented in mind-matter studies with REGs, also extends meaningfully into biology. Subtle yet dynamic relationships may connect all life. This controversial research, if it is valid, could have profound implications to our understandings of both biology and medicine.

There are many extraordinary claims to be found in the parapsychological literature, ranging from strange mystical experiences of individuals pronounced clinically dead and later resuscitated, to young children recalling memories of people who have lived before. I'm not sure what I think about these cases, of which there seem to be many, yet in view of what we can say critically about them, I think we must also accept that a movement toward an intrinsic view of consciousness potentially opens the possibility of phenomena we might have previously considered impossible. A skeptical yet open mind seems appropriate. We don't know what consciousness *is*, so how confident can we be, for example, that it is extinguished at death? I'm far from convinced that my personality and memories will survive the death of my physical body, but I must concede that a description of nature in which consciousness plays an important role is more favorable to notions of survival than ones in which it doesn't. A consequence of a more open-minded science is a greater awareness of what we don't know, especially with regard to consciousness. People's reported experiences take on greater significance. The existence of things once thought impossible may need to be reconsidered. Stepping away from the reductionist view of consciousness finds us on mysterious new terrain that we must struggle to find concepts to understand. To the extent to which we can embrace this larger unknown, our existing science may seem less powerful and encompassing, and yet if this is a more accurate appraisal of the state of our knowledge, so be it. A more humble science has nothing to loose and everything to gain.

We will shortly move away from the psi literature to consider compelling ideas about the place of mind in our larger cosmology. Before that, let's take a few moments here to reflect on where we've been and the road ahead. In investigating the hard problem of consciousness, we reviewed the inherent limits of explaining subjectivity within the prevailing reductive-materialistic approach. We explored how recognition of this has increasingly led respected thinkers to consider that consciousness reflects a fundamental aspect of the world. In philosophy we saw this view expressed in the form of the *intrinsic nature argument*, where we explored why some philosophers believe physics ultimately requires an experiential or proto mind-like underpinning in order to be complete. In venturing into neuroscience, we explored how the leading theory of consciousness in neuroscience today embraces a form of mathematical panpsychism – describing consciousness as an essential feature of information. We saw that this model, known as integrated information theory or 'IIT', has a mathematical basis capable of making testable predictions about the brain's structure and activity. In the new field of quantum biology we saw how quantum states are increasingly being identified to play significant roles in biological processes. In Penrose and Hameroff's quantum approach to consciousness, we considered that quantum processes, including entanglement, might play an important role in sentience. We then looked at how insights from modern physics are leading to new theories about the mind's relationship to the world, including the view that *information* rather than matter and energy lies at the foundations of physics. From here we explored an apparent role for consciousness that, in spite of a taboo, is believed by many prominent physicists to rest at the heart of quantum mechanics. Here, we saw that quantum systems behave in distinct ways that apparently depend on the information that can be made available to observers. Taking stock of this, we reviewed recent experiments pursuing a new and radical approach to this mystery. The results of experiments led by Dean Radin and his colleagues at IONS suggested that individuals with attentional training, such as experience with meditative practice, could successfully reduce the uncertainty of a quantum system when all other variables other than their attention were ruled out. There indeed seemed to be a psychic component to measurement. This led us to consider the growing consensus among psi researchers: that consciousness acts as a kind of ordering principle – rooted deeply in the organization of nature. Investigating this possibility, we examined a body of evidence contributed by several independent laboratories and research teams exploring how directed intention on the part of ordinary participants seems able to influence the behavior of sensitive physical systems. Surprisingly these effects were also reported in experiments both displaced in time, and carried out over large distances. The mental push of intentionality appeared to extend beyond the individual, dialoguing with the underlying order of the world. If these studies show what they appear to, then mind and world must be recognized to exist meaningfully within the same continuum. Scientists involved in this research suggested that these effects occur at a level of reality that antedates the distinction between observer and the observed. We then encountered the Global Consciousness Project. This on-going mind-matter experiment, led by psychologist Roger Nelson, reports that events capturing the attention of large populations around the planet correlate with the statistical order of a vast global network of sensitive physical instruments. This study, and the earlier experiments that justified it, have produced compelling evidence that seemingly separate minds coalesce when individuals share similar thoughts, feelings and emotions. This led us to clinical telepathy experiments, the findings of which suggest our minds may only ever be superficially separate from one another. We saw how this view has been further supported by a wealth of studies using the sensory depravation technique known as the ganzfeld. In light of mounting evidence, we considered the possibility that our minds exist as features within a single experiential system. The view that consciousness may be unbound by familiar causal constraints was further supported by experiments interrogating mind's relationship to time. We saw that laboratory studies suggest people's subconscious mind and physiological activity respond to yet-to-be-determined events. This research would seem to indicate that our minds exist in a dialogue with the flux of future potential events, just over the temporal horizon. Among various other compelling studies, we saw in experiments carried out by Daryl Bem, that well-known psychological processes can apparently be mirrored in time, capturing enigmatic evidence of 'memories' of the future.

The failure of current scientific paradigms to make sense of psi evidence is no reason to abandon scientific study of them. Indeed, Thomas Kuhn's concept of a scientific paradigm includes the necessity and inevitability of scientific revolutions.[6] As observed anomalies become increasingly salient, the prevailing paradigm approaches what Kuhn described as the 'crisis point,' at which time the epistemological geometry of science re-forms into a new structure, capable of comfortably explaining everything pragmatically demonstrated before, but now to shine light into a previously unrealized dimension of nature. At the crisis point there is a period of high creativity, where in the right place and at the right time, revolutionary ideas can ignite lasting change in the character of the debate. The realization that our world is a sphere, that species evolve and adapt, that physics follows mathematical logic – the history of science is marked by revolutionary ideas that opened our eyes to the world in new ways. The character of the looming realization; that the inner dimension of mind should occupy some intrinsic place in nature, seems yet more profound because now there is something about our most intimate being that is at stake.

We now find ourselves here, trying to reconcile a deeper view of consciousness with an understanding of the larger cosmic process. Could a new conception of reality accommodate these mysterious aspects of the mind? As we will now explore, the intrinsic consciousness movement can also be seen extending into cosmology. Here, decorated physicists offer intriguing ideas and theories about the place of mind in the larger cosmos. They point to a richer perspective that both reunites mind and world as well as potentially shedding new light on the deepest mysteries of existence. We will now consider the possibility of a more meaningful view of our place in the universe, our future, and the origins of consciousness.

'The architecture of the universe is consistent with the hypothesis that mind plays an essential role in its functioning.'[7]

Freeman Dyson
Physicist

10. THE MEANINGFUL UNIVERSE

Less than a century ago, the human understanding of the universe underwent an unprecedented expansion. In 1926, the astronomer Edwin Hubble discovered that our universe was much vaster than our Milky Way galaxy, and that many billions of others existed. We learned that each of these distant galaxies had an average of a hundred thousand millions stars. Many of them were much like our own, with orbiting planets and moons. We were almost certainly not the only life that had evolved in the vast cosmos, but in the eerie silence of space, Earth was a fragile speck, and humanity had never seemed so alone in its struggle to survive. As a species we began to wonder if we were as insignificant as we were small. Despite our humble size, however, there are compelling reasons to suggest that the emergence of life is far from irrelevant in the cosmic scheme of things. In fact, according to several prominent scientists and philosophers, it may play a fundamental role in the cycle of existence.

In the last century, as physicists turned powerful new technologies toward the skies, they looked further and deeper into the cosmos than anyone before them. As they applied rigorous mathematics to calculate the physical values governing the evolution of the universe, they developed ways to determine these parameters with ever-greater accuracy. Within this set of relationships, however, emerged an astonishing finding. The 'laws' that guided the evolution of the universe were so precise as to appear 'finely tuned' in favor of the evolution of life. Upward of twenty physical constants rested on a razor knife-edge, any change to which would have catastrophic results for the possibility of complex life of any kind evolving anywhere in the universe. As physicist David Deutsch reflected,

> 'Nudge one of these constants just a few percent in one direction, stars burn out within a million years of their formation, and there is no time for evolution. If we nudge it a few percent in the other direction, then no elements heavier than helium form. No carbon, no life. Not even any chemistry. No complexity at all.'[1]

In the late 20th century, physicists calculated a universal law known as the 'cosmological constant.' It refers to the value of the energy density in otherwise empty space. The cosmological constant acts weakly against the gravitational force and is responsible for the precise rate of expansion of the universe. The cosmologists studying it soon recognized that it had played a critical role in cosmic evolution. When it was calculated, however, they shrank from their findings. Alter this value in even the smallest way and, among other devastating consequences, stars would not ignite, heavy elements would not have formed, and any hopes for even the most imaginative notions of life are crushed. If nothing but randomness was at play, the chances of the cosmological constant having a life-friendly value are many trillions to one. Together, the universal laws and constants could have evolved within many multiples of trillions of intelligible arrangements, and yet only an impossible fraction of these could have supported life of any kind. As cosmologist Michael Turner once put it,

> 'The precision is as if one could throw a dart across the entire universe and hit a bull's eye one millimeter in diameter on the other side.'[2]

Somehow the universe supported the precise conditions to allow self-reflection on itself through living observers. What are we to make of this? Cosmologists respond to this mystery in several ways. Some offer a promissory note. Perhaps the cosmic laws are the way they are because they *need* to be like this. Maybe one day we will discover a grand unified theory that reveals that the laws governing the universe are not a set of purely random values, but instead, in their precise form, could not have been any other way. More or less, we live in the only possible universe. The drawback of this explanation is that it makes its life-friendly conditions the result of pure chance. Given how precisely universal laws need to be 'tuned' for life, as a product of mere coincidence this seems flatly untenable. Why should some metaphysical constraint over existence line up with such extraordinary precision with a life-fertile universe? This demands an explanation.

Today, perhaps the most popular response among cosmologists is to confidently brush the mystery aside. Of course the universe has to be life-friendly because we're here to observe it. The reason why the universe appears so finely tuned for life is explainable by the existence of a *multiverse*. This inconceivably vast domain is the genesis of trillions upon trillions of other universes. The chances of a life fertile universe may be impossibly small, but roll the dice a few trillion, trillion times and, sooner or later, you'll get lucky. The theory is reminiscent though distinct from the 'many worlds' interpretation of quantum mechanics, in which there is invoked a near infinity of worlds, just as real as our own, in which the possible outcomes of every quantum event are played out and granted full reality. In the multiverse theory we are asked to accept the existence of countless trillions of other universes, among which a comparatively tiny number exist that, through nothing but the outworking of chance, are fertile for the evolution of life and mind. Our concept of the universe has radically expanded before; perhaps we'll also have to recognize the existence of many trillions of other universes as well.

The multiverse may be a popular idea but there's far from any consensus among scientists regarding the theory's coherence. The physicist Paul Davies has documented a number of troubling issues with the multiverse hypothesis that may cause us to hesitate before embracing it.[3] Firstly, the multiverse would require a *universe-generating mechanism*, capable of producing trillions upon trillions of universes. It would also have to be able to produce and sustain the entire spectrum of their governing laws individually. This, Davies argues, would demand that the multiverse has its own precisely tuned universe-creating and maintaining laws. Rather than providing a more elegant explanation, the multiverse supposes something vastly complex. Multiverse theories presuppose important principles of both quantum mechanics and relativity, but do not offer any adequate explanation for how it came to acquire them. How did the multiverse, with its universe-generating mechanism, come into being? And is there just one multiverse or many? Like the religious claims about an intelligent creator, the multiverse theory also leads to questions that quickly spiral toward infinite regression. Davies likened the multiverse theory to the scientific equivalent of a creation myth, seeming almost as unbelievable as it is unprovable. But there is another reason to be cautious of any theory that appeals to outside of the universe in search of an explanation of its origins: As long as we choose to construct our description of the universe against the backdrop of some completely unknowable, transcendent exterior, we may forever deny the possibility of a more elegant self-consistent explanation, and in so doing, resign ourselves to never truly understanding the universe. Davies argues that we should first exhaust theories that do not appeal to something beyond the universe. And, because of its mysteriously life-friendly conditions, this entails we consider the real possibility that life and mind will turn out to occupy a fundamental place in the cosmic scheme of things.

THE PARTICIPATORY UNIVERSE

It is an astonishing fact about the universe that it has realized a capability of observing itself through living observers. Does the existence of conscious observers reveal something fundamental about the character of the universe? In the third chapter we encountered some of the reasons reputable physicists have argued quantum physics points to an intractable role for consciousness in physics. We also looked numerous psi studies that apparently supporting this idea.

We will now explore how thinkers of recent decades have attempted to extrapolate what such a place for consciousness in physics may entail for our understanding of the larger universe.

A bizarre implication of quantum mechanics was first identified by John Wheeler in 1978.[4] He realized that observations should not only establish the state of quantum particles at the instant of measurement, but in principle they should also resolve how they behaved in the past. We briefly touched on this curious aspect of quantum theory in chapters 3 and 4. Choosing to observe a quantum particle, Wheeler recognized, also ought to define how it had behaved at earlier junctions. He envisaged a new thought experiment, he called 'quantum post-selection' to prove it. It wasn't till three decades later, however, that new technology made the experiment possible. In 2015, a team of Australian physicists confirmed Wheeler's predictions, observing the post-selection effect in helium atoms. Quantum theory had once again challenged our common-sense view of the world, only to be later confirmed by experiment. 'It proves that measurement is everything' remarked contributing professor Andrew Truscott. 'At the quantum level, reality does not exist if you are not looking at it.' He went on, 'If one chooses to believe that the atom really did take a particular path or paths, then one has to accept that a future measurement is affecting the atom's past ... It was only when they were measured at the end of the journey that their wave-like or particle-like behavior was brought into existence.'[5] Decades before these laboratory demonstrations, Wheeler had already begun exploring the cosmological implications.

In a post-selection experiment, just as in the classic double-slit experiment, photons or any other subatomic particle are beamed toward two slits in a barrier. Those particles traveling through the slits collide with a screen that records their impact – as either having behaved as a probability wave or tiny particulate objects – depending on our choice to measure. The difference in a post-selection experiment is that we observe the particles only *after* they have travelled through the slits. Surprisingly, if we choose to measure the particles at this later point we find that we can determine how they behaved when they travelled through the slits – as either a particle or wave. Essentially our choice to observe (or as Wheeler preferred, *'participate'*) forces the particles to assume a defined state at an earlier time. In a bold observation Wheeler pointed out that the photons of distant starlight could also be captured within a cosmic-scale post-selection experiment. Light from a distant celestial object like a quasar, could be lensed around the gravitational field of a nearer massive object like a galaxy. The result is that photons from the quasar could reach observers on Earth from either one side of the galaxy or the other. Just as in the double-slit experiment, the wave function of the photons is distributed between all possible paths around the galaxy. Even at cosmic distances, the laws of quantum physics must hold true. And, just as with quantum post-selection in the laboratory, when we choose to measure this ancient light on Earth, we force the photons to resolve their path around the galaxy, billions of light-years away in the distant past. The recent verification of quantum post-selection confirmed that, in a very real sense, observations reach across time and space, to resolve something about the history of the present. It was here in the quantum, at the heart of the most powerful physical theory ever conceived, that Wheeler believed laid the clues to why the universe is so life-friendly.

> 'Acts of observer-participancy – via the mechanism of the delayed-choice experiment – in turn give tangible 'reality' to the universe not only now but back to the beginning.'[6]

But how could this be possible? How do we explain observers? The answer, for Wheeler, lay in recognizing the constants of nature, not as fixed and infinitely precise from the moment of the Big Bang, but emergent *with* the universe. Wheeler had conducted pioneering theoretical work with the now widely held view that quantum *information*, rather than matter and energy, constitutes the true foundations of nature. The laws of nature emerge from information, but if we unflinchingly accept quantum physics, observers must be understood to *create* information. Wheeler reasoned that only a physics capable of achieving 'observer participancy' could evolve.[7] The universe, he argued, must be understood as a single 'self-excited circuit' in which rather than passive observers, we are active *participators*. Modern physics tells us that, not only is the world based on a principle of uncertainty, even its history is still in the process of being resolved. Every observation refines down part of a consistent history of the present. Wheeler was keen to impress that it was the observer's *choice* to measure, rather than simply their employing measuring instruments, that was significant.

> 'Nothing is more important about the quantum principle than this, that it destroys the concept

of the world 'sitting out there', with the observer safely separated from it by a 20 centimeter slab of plate glass. Even to observe such a minuscule object as an electron, he must shatter the glass. He must reach in. He must install his chosen measuring equipment. It is up to him to decide whether he shall measure position or momentum. To install the equipment to measure the one prevents and excludes his installing the equipment to measure the other. Moreover, the measurement changes the state of the electron. The universe will never afterwards be the same. To describe what has happened, one has to cross out the old word 'observer' and put in its place the new word 'participator'. In some strange sense the universe is a participatory universe.'[8]

The influential physicist, Anton Zeilinger, who conducted groundbreaking research in quantum teleportation, praised Wheeler's willingness to confront the extraordinary implications of quantum mechanics without clinging to outdated mechanistic descriptions of nature, including what he described as 'the obviously wrong notion of a reality independent of us.'[9] The British cosmologist and astrophysicist, Sir Martin Rees confronted the strange logic of quantum post-selection when he wrote,

'In the beginning there were only probabilities. The universe could only come into existence if someone observed it. It does not matter that the observers turned up several billion years later. The universe exists because we are aware of it.'[10]

Earlier in his career, Wheeler expressed staunch criticism toward the possibility of any causal role of mind in nature. In 1979 he called for the Parapsychological Association to be removed from the American Association for the Advancement of Science. In a tirade against psi research he decried parapsychology as a pseudoscience, even accusing its founder, J.B. Rhine, of fraud. Later the same year he retracted the accusation, which he admitted was groundless. Wheeler stood by his rejection of the field, yet despite his misgivings, his work explored the same possibility driving psi research – that the observing mind plays an intrinsic, participatory role in the world. Derived from the implications of quantum mechanics, his ideas had unmistakably begun circling a once-heretical notion: a seemingly teleological link between the origins of the universe and the evolution of life and mind. As Wheeler put it,

> '[The participator] gives the world the power to come into being, through the very act of giving meaning to that world; in brief, 'No consciousness; no communicating community to establish meaning? Then no world!' 'On this view, the universe is to be compared to a circuit self-excited in this sense, that the universe gives birth to consciousness, and consciousness gives meaning to the universe.'[11]

This image is based on drawings used by Wheeler in his lectures on the participatory universe.

The idea that information may have a subjective as well as an objective pole is a basic tenet of Tononi's integrated information theory of consciousness. As we explored earlier, despite being a form of panpsychism, it is now among the leading theories of consciousness in neuroscience today. A competing theory, Hameroff and Penrose's Orch-OR, which also calls for a form of panpsychism, attributes consciousness to the information created during the collapse of quantum states in the brain. As we move toward a view of physics as both informational and nonlocal, it seems at least possible that a future theory will bridge elements of IIT and Orch-OR, perhaps shedding light on our mysterious conscious participation with quantum reality.

On March 17th 2014, media cameras captured the moment when physicist Andrei Linde was greeted at his front door by an excited colleague. Linde was overwhelmed to hear the news that his predictions about the early universe, billionths of a second after the Big Bang, had recently been supported by new measurements of the cosmic background radiation. It was an emotional moment for the father of inflation theory, and he and his wife toasted his success with Champagne in their kitchen. While Linde is a widely known and highly respected scientist, he has been frank about what he considers to be the potentially fundamental place of consciousness in the establishment of physical reality. In a contribution to a 2002 book honoring John Wheeler's 90th birthday, Linde urged his colleagues to keep an open mind toward a place for consciousness in physics. Everything we know about existence, after all, occurs through acts of perception. 'Could it be' he wrote, 'that consciousness is an equally important part of the consistent picture of our world, despite the fact that so far one could safely ignore it in the description of the well-studied physical processes? Will it not turn out, with the further development of science, that the study of the universe and the study of consciousness are inseparably linked, and that ultimate progress in the one will be impossible without progress in the other?'[12] According to

Linde, despite its potential for misuse, there are compelling reasons to consider that consciousness plays a fundamental role in quantum measurement. 'Avoiding the concept of consciousness in quantum cosmology', he warned, 'may lead to an artificial narrowing of our outlook.'[13] Linde is among a number of physicists that have pointed out that the quantum wave function of the entire universe could not evolve in time without the introduction of a relative observer. He argued for the possibility of other universes and that indeed a multiverse of sorts might exist, but he also voiced his suspicions that consciousness may play a fundamental role in their realization.[14] Advancing on these ideas, Paul Davies recently considered the possibility that all such 'self-excited loops' might exist.[15] This view, while somewhat reminiscent of the traditional multiverse theory, has the benefit of making every possible universe internally self-explanatory. It takes seriously both the apparently intractable role of observers in the evolution of quantum systems, and the otherwise miraculous emergence of consciousness from unconscious matter. It removes the necessity of a complex universe-generating mechanism occupying a transcendent multiverse, because each self-excited universe self-generates its own laws. As we will consider shortly, it may also shed light on that age-old question: Why is there something rather than nothing? But, if as quantum mechanics suggests, observations resolve something about the past, then observations made in the distant future should also resolve something about the reality we experience in the present. This brought into question the far future of observers in the universe. Given enough time, just what feats might be achievable by life and mind on the cosmic stage? Is there an ultimately realized universe that lies ahead of us? Could it be, as David Deutsch imagined, that,

> 'At the end of time, life will have spread throughout space, it will have gained control of all matter and all forces, and it will have acquired all knowledge there is to know.'[16]

Several physicists have considered that the destiny of life is to saturate the entire cosmos, resulting in a universe that eventually achieves 'closure' by becoming what Davies described as 'completely self-known.' And if this is so,

> '...then the whole character of the universe, including the emergence of its laws and the nature of its states become inextricably intertwined with its mentality – with its *mindfulness*.'[17]

Does, over the course of billions of years of evolution, life satisfy a cosmic imperative that in some way contributes to the integrity of the entire system? Does the realization of a universe depend for its existence on processes intrinsic to life and mind? It need hardly be stated that we are now well into the realm of speculation, yet as extraordinary as such a view might sound, as we will now explore, several prominent thinkers are convinced of its merit.

THE COSMIC IMPERATIVE

In two short centuries our species made extraordinary advancements in science and technology. We cured diseases, walked on the Moon, sent probes to other planets and realized the existence of a global internet. Advancing the timeline forwards, hundreds, thousands, millions, even billions of years, unimaginable feats may be achievable by life on the cosmic stage. Life may be extraordinarily adaptable, yet its continued survival on Earth has always been in question. Earth life has faced the threat of total extinction many times. Ninety nine percent of all species that ever lived are now extinct. Scientists warn that we are currently in the midst of the sixth mass extinction of life on Earth. There is no guarantee that our species will prove capable of adapting quick enough to survive the impact of our own crushing weight on the biosphere. It has become ever more apparent that the continued survival of the entire Earth genus of life rests in the hands of just one or two generations. However, even if our own fate is so precarious, we will almost certainly not be the last word from life on the cosmic stage. The universe, we know, is rich with the elements for biological life. Even if we take the view that life is exceedingly rare, and among habitable planets and moons, it arises spontaneously just once in every 10 million fertile environments, the universe would yet be teaming with life, occupying billions of worlds. As Senior Astronomer of California's SETI Institute, Seth Shostak pointed out,

> 'The number of habitable worlds in our galaxy is certainly in the tens of billions, minimum, and we haven't even talked about the moons. And

the number of galaxies we can see, other than our own, is about 100 billion.'[18]

If just a tiny fraction of these produce life, and just a fraction of those produce *intelligent* life, the likelihood is that there are millions upon millions of intelligent civilizations in the known universe. It would take only a precious few of these to gain the ability to safely navigate between stars for a galactic community to spring forth. Such a community, no longer dependent on the relative fragility of its local home and star system, would stand a much greater chance of continued survival. The more widely distributed and technologically capable, the less chance unforeseen events will lead to its extinction. Beyond a certain stage of vulnerable adolescence, such as that in which we find ourselves today, the continued survival of any advanced civilization greatly increases. On a cosmic timeline, the longer that life survives, the more the odds are stacked in its favor. Even if the majority of life is destined to destroy itself, several thinkers have taken the view that it is a virtual statistical certainty that life and mind will eventually saturate the entire universe.

In recent years, the world renowned futurist and inventor Raymond Kurzweil has stimulated academic and popular discussion with his predictions of a 'technological singularity.'[19] Based on the observed trend that computational power consistently doubles approximately every year, Kurzweil points to a time – just decades ahead, in which technological advancement approaches a point of exponential acceleration. Beyond this silicon Rubicon, what lies ahead for humanity defies our ability to predict with accuracy, and yet Kurzweil believes that relatively soon, humans may gain the ability to extend life indefinitely, radically upgrade our intelligence and even reshape human nature. Ultimately we may even leave our biological origins behind completely, creating synthetic avatar forms that transcend the constraints of our fragile bodies. The controversial ideas of Kurzweil and his supporters in the transhumanist movement have increasingly penetrated the cultural zeitgeist and now many look ahead toward a time, possibly within their own lifetime, in which a technological leap galvanizes an extraordinary future. While there are those skeptical about just how imminent any 'singularity' may be, most agree that technology will continue to dramatically change our lives and the world around us. Beyond these more short-term predictions, Kurzweil has also looked far ahead toward the role of intelligent life in the universe at large. He argues that cosmologists routinely under appreciate the extraordinary potential of an evolving intelligence to restructure the entire cosmos.

> 'Intelligence is very powerful. It is the most powerful force that we are aware of. Intelligence can overcome [supposed] natural limits – not through any kind of magic, but just by figuring ways to manipulate forces at finer and finer scales so that, ultimately, what seem to be natural limits can be superseded. It won't take that long for us to do this at a solar-system scale and then a galaxy-wide scale. Ultimately, we will turn the universe into a large mind that is trillions of trillions of times greater than all of human intelligence today.'[2]

Does mind and consciousness satisfy a form of cosmic imperative? Could it be that the ultimate destiny of intelligence in the universe is in some way connected to its origin? Kurzweil doesn't explicitly allude to this possibility, but several thinkers have. Freeman Dyson is a decorated theoretical physicist famous for his predictions about life's future in the cosmos. He is perhaps best known for his concept of the *Dyson sphere*: a spherical artificial megastructure large enough to encompass and harvest the energy of an entire star. Such structures, Dyson believes, may be required to satisfy the extraordinary energy requirements of a burgeoning technological civilization. He advised that, in their search for extra-terrestrial life, astronomers should look for these structures, which may be visible in star's emitting anomalous wavelengths of light for their known stellar type. Dyson considered that the emergence of life could be highly significant, not just for understanding the destiny of the energy in the universe, but also its origin and primordial structure.

> 'It is conceivable that life may have a larger role to play than we have yet imagined. Life may succeed against all the odds in molding the universe to its own purposes. And the design of the inanimate universe may not be as detached from the potentialities of life and intelligence as scientists of the 20th century have tended to suppose.'[21]

Perhaps mind and consciousness serve as a vehicle to comprehension the universe in some way requires. In the philosopher Teilhard de Chardin's most famous work, *The Human Phenomenon*, he envisaged life and mind as engaged in a greater cosmic evolutionary process.[22] According to Teilhard, the course of life is naturally driven to ever-advancing complexity, consciousness and intelligence – the ultimate state of which, perhaps billions of years in the future, approaches a cosmic singularity of infinite complexity and consciousness. This future attractor was the inevitable realization of a cosmic imperative, necessary in satisfying the conditions of its own creation. Teilhard called this singularity the *Omega Point*, and while his ideas were certainly influenced by his Christian faith, other secular thinkers have considered life's unique ability to transform its environment, and that in a still mysterious way, may have also shaped its origins. Intelligence, as it arises in us, and almost certainly in many other places in the universe, permits the evolution of an experiential, cognitive dimension through which reality comes to know about itself. Through conscious life, the universe creates the unique opportunity to become *self-realizing*. Davies has suggested that, over trillions of years:

> '...matter will be used to process information and create a rich mental world, perhaps without limit. Many scientists have speculated that, as the timeline stretches towards infinity, so an emerging super-intelligence will become more and more god-like, so that in the final stage, the super-mind will merge with the universe: mind and cosmos will be one.'[23]

Any low-orbit view of Earth's surface reveals life's explicit restructuring of matter. Psi research suggests the existence of a deeper relationship between mind and world. Experiments such as those conducted at Princeton's PEAR laboratory seemed to show that the activity of mind introduces order into the world, even when everything but attention and intention is removed from the equation.[24] Consciousness appears to exist in an intimate dialogue with reality – that changes in the 'order' of consciousness are reflected in changes in the order of the world. Where attention goes, order mysteriously flows.

The world-renowned neuroscientist Christof Koch has been a vocal supporter of Tononi's integrated information theory of consciousness. When, during an interview, he was asked to comment on the mysterious fine-tuning of the universe for life and mind, he agreed that the laws of physics do seem to give rise to a universe that inextricably births complexity. Koch maintained that this complexity, as it tends toward ever-greater degrees of integration, gives rise to ever-greater degrees of consciousness. He suggested that this natural process, as it is now occurring on Earth, will eventually extend meaningfully into our technology, and ultimately toward the 'global, planetary wide consciousness imagined by Teilhard De Chardin.'[25]

The traditional conception of the universe is that all order is slave to, and ultimately the victim of *entropy* – the second law of thermodynamics that holds that all thermodynamic systems will tend toward disorder. It predicts that eventually, all stars will die, all structure will decay, and finally, after trillions of years, there will be nothing but a cold, featureless void. This is sometimes referred to as the 'heat death' of the universe. Far from a climactic cosmic self-actualization, the universe may have a more depressing fate. Certainly the mathematics of entropy cannot be refuted, and yet the universe we see around us is staggeringly more complex than it has ever been. Historically the universe has only become more complex. It is populated by a rich panoply of phenomena, including galaxies, stars, planets, life and consciousness. This increasing complexity is not easily reconciled with the second law, and is known as the 'problem of entropy'. Can we rule out that another kind of force exists, perhaps reminiscent of gravity, which draws phenomena toward greater and greater complexity? As we have explored, there is a wealth of experiments using random event generators (also known as maximum entropy systems) that point toward an enigmatic relationship between the coherence of minds and the order of the world. A new understanding may yet lie ahead of us, in which entropy and consciousness are recognized as counterbalancing cosmic forces, both necessary in the cosmic dance through which the universe comes into being. The laws of thermodynamics are at work in every living cell. Without entropy at play in the fundamental processes of biology, life could never have evolved. Perhaps, then, entropy is required to give the universe the freedom to evolve, but is ultimately destined to fall under the burgeoning purchase of life and mind over physics.

Physicists devoted to the search for a theory of everything sometimes talk excitedly about the possibility of an equation elegant enough to fit on the front of a T-shirt. Such a formula has been viewed as the Holy Grail of theoretical physics. Einstein spent much of his life in search of it. However, even if such a formula could be found, as Stephen Hawking famously pointed out, there would still be the question of what it is that 'breathes fire' into this equation to give rise to the real, living universe in which we find ourselves.[26] This relates closely to that other most ancient and perennial mystery: why is there anything at all? What primordial rational ground required existence, and what is its nature? For the answer to avoid being endlessly recursive – always simply adding to our picture of existence and thus adding to that we are hoping to explain, it cannot describe any physical kind of thing in the ordinary sense. The ultimate ground of being, it seems, must be self-subsuming – containing within itself its own explanation. David Chalmers recently proposed that, due to its apparently nonphysical qualities, consciousness may constitute the necessarily existing ground – that which realizes and gives reality to the laws of physics.[27] He tentatively suggested that a deeper understanding of reality's self-realizing nature could entail its being inherently experiential. This would give force to the *intrinsic nature argument* we encountered in chapter two; in which it seems required that the intrinsic nature of reality is more mind-like than classically physical.

The idea that the question of consciousness invades the question of existence is far from a recent notion. In the late 18th and early 19th centuries, a movement in philosophy known as *German idealism* rose to prominence in Europe. As the movement progressed, a core circle of thinkers argued for the absolute primacy of consciousness. Among notable other philosophers, Johann Fichte, Friedrich Schelling and Wilhelm Hegel urged that a deeper understanding of consciousness would be necessary to understand why anything exists at all. It was Schelling, however, that identified a direct parallel with the absolute ground of existence and the essential structure of consciousness. The ground of being, from which all existence flows, can only be being itself. It must thus be self-grounding – existing only in the context of itself. Schelling observed that this strange circularity is a quality otherwise unique to consciousness. As Fichte his contemporary had argued, consciousness is not grounded in anything beyond itself. The conscious self is its own 'posit' – self-producing in so far that it exists only in and to itself. Other philosophers have since observed this circular self-realizing aspect of consciousness. As Jean-Paul Sartre remarked, '… it is the very nature of consciousness to exist in a circle.'[28] Another philosopher, Douglas Hofstadter observed that, 'It is almost as if this slippery phenomenon called 'self-consciousness' lifted itself up by its own bootstraps, almost as if it made itself out of nothing.'[29] It was precisely these qualities that Schelling identified as necessary attributes of the ultimate ground of existence. Furthermore, he argued, they could be found nowhere else but in consciousness. Schelling reasoned that the universe existed because it 'posits itself' and thus, in its most essential nature, is experiential. The contemporary philosopher Freya Mathews argues a similar position to Schelling, observing that any self-causing principle behind the universe must be *reflexive*, meaning that it directs back into itself.[30] This self-causing principle behind the universe, observes Mathews, requires the intentional attribute of being 'about itself' that is found nowhere else but in the mental. It may be, for all we know, a brute metaphysical fact that existence has intrinsic value over non-existence, and that some kind of intentional closure is necessary in its realization. The view that existence must have intrinsic value is a position with philosophical roots stretching all the way back to Plato. More recently, in his *Value and Existence,* the philosopher John Leslie argued that the question of existence ultimately and unavoidably reduces to a question of intrinsic *value.*[31] The concept of value, as Nagel has also observed, is a concept that has its occasion within consciousness alone. If the universe involves value, it must also involve consciousness. Mathews points out that an intrinsic view of consciousness also seems to make light of a number of otherwise intractable mysteries about the deep structure of reality. For example, from the standard materialist perspective, it must be regarded as pure metaphysical fortuity that the universe hangs together as a coherent unity. The indivisible unity of consciousness, if it is an intrinsic feature of reality, may form part of the explanation. Elsewhere Davies considers that it could be a highly significant fact about the universe that it produces thinking beings potentially capable of understanding it. By introducing intelligibility to the universe life ultimately allows a means through which the universe can, in a particular sense, be self-explanatory. A self-consistent account of the universe, he suggests, might also necessitate that it be self-explanatory and as such, produce beings capable of explaining it.[32]

THE PRINCIPLE OF CHOICE

Our consciousness seems to be more than in passive attendance to our thoughts; we have the experience of making free choices, with purposes and goals. Consciousness *feels* like it is in control. As philosopher John Searle is fond of saying, 'I decide consciously to raise my arm, and the damn thing goes up!'[33]

The problem is that our apparent ability to make free choices seems to be in direct conflict with a common-sense view of the universe. If our choices are the result of a causal chain of physical events, leading into the past and out of our control, to what extent can we really have freewill? It is a seemingly unavoidable fact that straightforward arguments demonstrate that the kind of freewill we imagine ourselves to have could not possibly exist within a deterministic material universe. The freedom of our actions would need to somehow transcend the causal precedence of prior states of the brain. A deterministic material universe seems to leave no room for true freedom. Whilst our consciousness cannot be doubted, perceptions can be. Illusions of all kinds make this clear. Just as our perceptions misled our ancestors into believing the world is flat, might we be wrong that we have freewill? Mainstream theories of consciousness have failed to convincingly explain the function consciousness plays in life. If it is an illusion, it cannot play any role in our brains, let alone the physical world. With the same strokes that materialist approaches reduce consciousness to an illusion, they are also forced to forfeit freewill. Matters get worse when we see that the basic fact that we make free choices is also incompatible with *philosophical realism* – the view that a purely objective world exists independently of observers.

In the 20th century, several attempts were made to understand freewill by virtue of the fact that the quantum world is governed by statistical probabilities rather than a deterministic chain of events. Because it is impossible to predict with certainty when and where quantum events will happen, in a certain sense, nature herself doesn't know what will happen next. Some philosophers put forward the case that because nature is ultimately governed by chance and not determinism, there is permitted the necessary wriggle room for freewill. The stumbling point of this approach, however, turns out to be the same as that which was initially problematic about determinism: It makes our choices the result of causal processes beyond our control. Introducing uncertain or random processes – which are also by definition outside of our control, doesn't seem to leave us in a better situation. The existence of freewill seems to demand that our conscious center of agency originates somehow outside of space and time. This is the end of the line for most mainstream thinkers, yet as we have seen, the evidence of psi apparently suggests just this – that the origins of consciousness are rooted to a domain of nature preceding the emergence of space and time. Furthermore, our most advanced physics now apparently refutes philosophical realism too. In a mysterious way, measurement and observation themselves define the behavior of the subatomic world. If consciousness is, as Chalmers suggests, the 'M property' – causing quantum collapse, then an active 'role' for consciousness is preserved at the very heart of nature. How exactly we are to understand this, though, is far from clear. With characteristic ingenuity, Freeman Dyson reframed the discussion when he considered that *choice*, rather than chance might be a fundamental feature of nature.

> 'Matter in quantum mechanics is not an inert substance but an active agent, constantly making choices between alternative possibilities. ... It appears that mind, as manifested by the capacity to make choices, is to some extent inherent in every electron.'[34]

Could it be that *choice*, and not randomness, lies at the heart of quantum uncertainty? Perhaps the problems we encounter when trying to explain freewill are the result of the assumption that the activities of consciousness are a product of their associated material processes rather than an intrinsic animating feature of them. A certain freedom permitted the universe to exist. This mysterious cosmic unfolding represents the exercising of a kind of freedom we do not yet understand. Maybe our own freewill is an extention of this same freedom. If our consciousness is truly a participatory aspect of the universal evolutionary process, instead of having freewill, perhaps it is truer to say that freedom has us.

TELOS AND COSMOS

A central reason that mainstream scientists tend to reject the idea of a universe driven toward life and mind is that it is *teleological* – it implies that nature is meaningful and purposive rather than blind to future outcomes. Individuals from a wide range of religious faiths have attempted to appropriate the apparent fine-tuning of the universe as evidence supporting their convictions in a supernatural creator. Many scientists are cautious of giving any credence to these ideas. It seems like a dangerous step toward giving validation to human superstitions and what is often perceived as the negative influence of religion in our world. However, a cosmic imperative toward life and consciousness, while often taken as such, does not necessarily entail the existence of an omnipotent creator being. If the destiny of the universe is bound up with its origins, we may need to recognize the existence of *future attractors* – forces in nature that pull. As several reputable thinkers have argued, a form of indwelling 'natural', rather than 'supernatural' teleology may be required to account for life's existence in the universe.

In his provocative 2012 book, *Mind and Cosmos*, the philosopher Thomas Nagel argued that the inability to reduce the mental to the physical casts shadows of uncertainty on standard materialism's ability to explain even the inanimate world. Nothing about the current conception of evolution predicts that conscious beings should, or could emerge. This, for Nagel, prompts serious doubts on its efficacy as a complete theory of life. One of the most astonishing things about mind is not merely its presence in living things, but its engagement with purposive and goal-directed behavior. No satisfying philosophical argument seems capable of neutralizing this. Furthermore, intentions – as characterized by the ability to both think about things and form and pursue goals, Nagel argues, cannot be intelligently separated from the reality of conscious experience. The undeniable existence of goals in ourselves poses a real challenge to a view of nature as essentially blind to future possibilities. We, at least, who are a part of nature, are not. According to Nagel, the rise of mind in the universe poses such a challenge to our ordinary reductive mechanistic view that a complete understanding of evolution may ultimately require us to embrace a form of 'natural teleology' – inherent predispositions in nature that tend toward certain outcomes.

Scholars have typically associated teleological views with the will of an all-powerful creator, yet Nagel rejects this common notion that the one implies the other. Rather than imposed from the outside, nature may have its own indwelling creative impulse that not only explains why life and mind evolve, but may ultimately be necessary in understanding why anything at all exists. Nagel argues that there is nothing metaphysically incoherent, nor implicitly theological about a teleological cosmology. 'I have been persuaded', he writes, 'that the idea of teleological laws is coherent, and quite different from the idea of explanation of the intentions of a purposive being.' [35] While evolution is certainly driven by survival mechanisms playing out over the course of many generations, to be inclusive of the basic facts of consciousness and the purposive activity of organisms, Nagel argues that our evolutionary model may require the concomitant understanding as probing toward certain value conditions, among which, he speculates, is ever greater and complexifying consciousness. In the company of several historical and contemporary philosophers, Nagel argued that the question of existence – why there is a universe at all, ultimately reduces beyond physics to a question of its intrinsic value. As John Leslie has reflected, it must somehow be 'good' that the universe exists. In a similar line of thought Nagel argued that consciousness, which is the only known vehicle of value, might thus have been written into the cosmic code from the beginning.

> The teleological hypothesis is that these things may be determined not merely by value-free chemistry and physics but also by something else, namely a cosmic predisposition to the formation of life, consciousness, and the value that is inseparable from them.[36]

Nagel's tone was tentative throughout the book. He was careful to modestly situate his ideas within the current limits of human knowledge. Exactly how and why the universe brought forth life and mind he didn't know, and he suspected that it could be a long time before we do, and yet some form of natural teleology would almost certainly be necessary to account for the basic fact of consciousness, the goal-directed activities of life, and the extraordinarily finely tuned cosmic conditions that permit its flourishing. The ultimate evolutionary potential of life and mind may turn out to be intrinsic to the integrity of existence as we know it. Life and mind contribute to a mental dimension of the universe, and it could be far from inconsequential that in them, reality allows for the means of being self-knowing. In view of this, Nagel invites us to consider our lives as 'part of the lengthy process of the universe gradually waking up and becoming aware of itself.'[37]

The possibility that the universe is inherently driven toward life and consciousness was also explored in cultural historian Robert Wright's best selling book, *Nonzero*.[38] Wright argued that *cooperation* was a universal principle, inevitably born out through the course of natural selection. Organisms like us are ecosystems, comprised of trillions of cells. Evolution brought them together and united them in common needs. We are each of us thriving communities, examples of the extraordinary cooperation born out by evolution. Wright argued that as life evolves, this cooperative activity gradually extends beyond the organism to create increasing mutual interdependence. He observed that all evolution has an inherent propensity to take advantage of ever widening and complex cooperative behaviors he called 'non-zero sum games'. He borrowed this term from *game theory*; developed in the 1940s by physicist John von Neumann, who developed game theory as a method of reducing decision-making and strategy to their raw mathematical elements.[39] Wright argued that the dynamics of game theory ultimately lie behind all human and animal behavior. He contrasted positive-sum games – where cooperation leads to net gains overall, with negative-sum games – where there must be winners and losers and overall gains typically amount to zero. The rise of culture, art, language, agriculture, and technology were all the fruits of life's propensity to engage in positive-sum games. Even wars, where sides come together to engage a common enemy, are examples of a positive-sum game, albeit in the context of a larger zero-sum situation. However, as human societies become increasingly interdependent through the widening and complexifying of positive-sum interactions, opposing sides and their conflicts inevitably dissolve into mutually dependent cooperation. Wright argued that life, be it through human beings or any other organism that takes up the mantle of culture, if it can survive long enough, is ultimately driven toward unity. Moreover, this process, driven by the logic of game theory, seems woven into the very mathematics governing the laws of physics.

Wright, like several other thinkers, observes that the existence of consciousness is unpredicted by our standard materialism, which, he argues, predicts at best only a world populated by mindless zombies.[40] Furthermore, the existence of consciousness introduces real value and moral meaning into the world. Without consciousness, nothing would matter. In recognizing conscious experience as the only known vehicle for value, Wright is in agreement with other thinkers that value could be a necessary condition of existence.

Wright points out that life seems to bear hallmarks of goal-driven, teleological behavior. It engages in what he describes as 'flexible directionality through information processing'. In other words, it pursues goals and intelligently responds to changing environmental conditions. Wright, like Nagel, pointed out that humans and animals engage in distinct intentional behaviors with clear goals – a real problem if goals cannot exist. Neither Wright nor Nagel speak about psi, yet if we accept the evidence of mind-matter interaction research, then intentions must be recognized to have real currency in the order of the world. Such receptivity between mind and world only seems possible within a physics with an intrinsic mental aspect. If there is a current to evolution, perhaps toward greater consciousness, we might think of our own intentions and goals as expressions of it. They can struggle against the flow of the river, and yet sooner or later everything in its current is drawn in the same direction. But this is not a perfect analogy – *risk* is involved in life. Wright offers the example of a poppy seed. Evolution may have instilled the poppy seed with the 'goal' of growing into a poppy, and yet it might be destined to end up on a bagel. Just so, Wright tentatively suggested that the blossoming of Earth's rich biosphere is a product of a form of higher-order natural selection.[41] Earth life may yet fail to survive and seed other planets. We may, for example, irreparably damage the biosphere, or fall victim to a wayward comet, and yet life, wherever it emerges, may be predisposed toward a greater purpose among the stars. Curtailing any overstatement of what such a 'higher purpose' might be, he reflected,

> 'Higher purpose needn't be very high. If evolution indeed has a purpose, that purpose may, for all we know, be imbued not by a divinity, but by some amoral creative process.'[42]

Evolution may seem merciless at times; when predators rise to dominance, and terrible acts of prejudice leave deep scars in cultural memories, and yet the same governing logic of game theory also cultivates, and ultimately preferences cooperation, altruism and moral progress. We may not live in the kind of universe attended by an omnipotent being, who steps in to stop appalling tragedies befalling innocent people, and yet for Wright, the universal process seems to be imbued with a larger meaning: a process in which the evolution of consciousness plays an important, yet still mysterious role.

Wright's views were influential to Martin Seligman, the founder of positive psychology. Seligman, then holding the position of president of the *American Psychological Association*, considered that if evolution does indeed inherently follow the logic of game theory, it should have played a formative role in the evolution of our psychology. He reflected on the enduring enigma of why humans evolved to have pleasurable emotions or 'positive affect'. It seemed that simple negative affect avoidance could, at least in principle, have been employed by evolution to evoke all survival-based behavior. So, why do we experience positive emotion? 'Why' Seligman asked, 'has evolution given us a system of pleasant feelings right on top of a system of unpleasant feelings?'[43] Positive emotions, Seligman considered, may have evolved as a signaling system to inform us that we are engaged in a positive-sum game. Correspondingly, negative emotions evolved as a warning that a behavior could have a potentially negative-sum outcome. Both Seligman and Wright projected the creative and unifying potential of life and mind into the far, far future, to consider that all meaning may be captured within the arc of a much greater cosmic evolutionary process. This process, over cosmic scales of time, is moving toward an inconceivable state – the total self-actualization of the universe. More plausible than a universe that comes into existence from nowhere for no reason was, in Seligman's words, 'a god that comes at the end.'

The existence of consciousness is a profound mystery, eclipsed only by the mystery of existence itself. Could it be that these two mysteries are deeply connected? By learning about one can we reveal insights about the other? Today cosmologists locate the origins of the universe in a singularity 13.8 billion years ago in the 'Big Bang.' Today there are compelling hints that the Big Bang and the ultimate destiny of the universe are really one primordial singularity of existence, and that our relative spatiotemporal reference frame creates their apparent duality. To an incredulous scientific establishment, several scientists and philosophers now bravely suggest that life and mind have an important role to play in the universe. Our primary identity, they offer, is the slowly widening aperture of a mental dimension through which the universe is waking up.

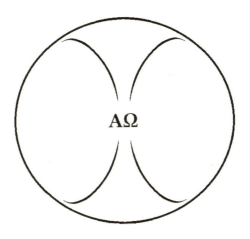

Are the origin and destiny of the universe one
primordial singularity of existence?

11. HORIZONS

The Copernican revolution, as it is sometimes called, was both a time of great revelation and profound existential uncertainty. As the new sun-centered model became more generally accepted, it brought into focus how unquestioned faith in religious doctrine could lead us astray from the truth. This sudden realization of the fallibility of our religious texts shook our once proud beliefs in our divinely bestowed centrality in the universe, and with it our cherished identity as the creation of an all-powerful being. The Copernican revolution catalyzed a new drive to understand the world beyond the hubris of our once naïve sense of significance. In the scientific revolution of the 17th and 18th centuries, Newton and other visionaries brought into view an understanding of nature as deterministically governed by unchanging physical laws. Initially this mechanistic worldview was vitalistic. While the behavior of physical objects and processes apparently lent themselves well to a full understanding through the interplay of deterministic forces, the purposive complexities of life seemed to stand distinctly apart from them. Life was thought to be animated by the energetic flowing through matter of an intrinsic vital spirit. As the German philosopher Immanuel Kant famously remarked, 'There will never be a Newton of the grassblade.'[1] However, in 1859, this common thought was dramatically overturned by Charles Darwin's evolutionary theory of life. It suddenly became obvious among many academic circles that the human being, once thought to be the subject of unique divine favor, was in fact, continuous with all other life. Our highly complex form had been born of an unimaginable number of blind iterations from simpler life. As life itself began to look as though it had a simple origin, the apparent need for a purposive creative intelligence was quickly receding. As their archetypal metaphor of the universe shifted from that of a great mind to a great machine, thinkers increasingly sought a mechanistic understanding of everything, including all vital and mental phenomena. In the cold light of day, all experience, memory and intention were increasingly thought of as identical with the complex, mechanistically determined activity of the human nervous system. While in philosophical discourse there were many notable countercurrents, as the centuries advanced, mind was increasingly perceived as an illusion. As a result, all meaning, value and purpose became reduced to mere human categories. Instead of ensouled beings, science communicators cast us as nothing but biological robots. There was no living spark separating us from the dead, inert, and nonexperiential outer matrix of matter. There was nothing 'special' about life, or the universe it inhabits, which was, in all likelihood, inherently absurd. Our sun, we learned, was a fairly typical star, inhabiting the outer reaches of the Milky Way, adrift in a cosmic sea of a hundred billion other galaxies. At once in awe of the vastness and beauty of the universe, our view of our place within it hardened as any special significance of humanity, or larger meaning of any kind, receded from our cosmic perspective.

The extraordinary power of science to grasp the causal structure of the world seemed to remove any apparent need for a reality beyond that which could be fully captured in deterministic material terms. Metaphysics – the study of the ultimate source and nature of existence, became increasingly marginalized. In the centuries following the scientific revolution, philosophy grew ever more analytical and subservient to science's strictly objective approach. However, by the turn of the 20th century, just as materialism was reaching the height of its dominance, clouds had unmistakably begun forming on the horizon. Our standard scientific worldview not only failed to explain the most certainly real aspect of the world: our consciousness, under new scrutiny the traditional grounded and concrete notions of matter upon which it was based were coming undone. As physicists developed the means to probe finer scales of nature, their familiar concepts of physicality, certainty, locality and time ceased to conform to their commonsense. Reality's seemingly concrete foundations had been an illusion. The emerging physics reintroduced an apparent necessity for metaphysics. The world it described was an unseen realm of potential out of which the classical world mysteriously coalesced. In this deeply interconnected and holistic reality, notions of *choice*, *information* and *knowledge* emerged as indispensable concepts. Beginning with the founders of quantum theory, many thinkers began to believe that, in order to be complete, an essentially subjective aspect would need to be introduced to our physical description of the world. A strictly objective science, they argued, could only take us so far.

In light of this, and the growing recognition of the philosophical significance of consciousness, toward the latter half of the 20th century, a resurgence of philosophers argued for the necessity of an intrinsic view of mentality. The inability to reduce it to physical processes – the 'hard' problem, suggested that, like the 'two' sides of a Möbius strip, the experiential and the physical are inseparable aspects of a single underlying nature. In related lines of thought, others argued that the necessary qualities required to describe the intrinsic nature of matter are unique to those interior qualities of consciousness. Other academics, returning to strands of thought first discussed three centuries earlier by European philosophers, observed that the uniquely self-realizing and self-grounding aspects of consciousness seem also to be necessary properties of the self-generating ground of existence. Indeed, for a small though growing number of contemporary philosophers the issue of consciousness cuts at the roots of our scientific ontology, with implications to our entire understanding of the physical world. 'The mind-body problem', writes Nagel, 'is not just a local problem, having to do with the relation between mind, brain and behavior in living animal organisms ... it invades our understanding of the entire cosmos and its history.'[2] In neuroscience recent years have seen the question of consciousness surge with new interest. Increasing numbers of thinkers have approached the view that, rather than an illusion, consciousness is real, and understanding it will require our exploring new avenues that go beyond the eliminative reductionist approaches of past decades. Among other compelling new theories taking an intrinsic view of consciousness, recent years saw much mainstream attention surrounding Tononi's integrated information theory, which has arguably risen to the leading theory of consciousness in neuroscience today. Despite being a form of panpsychism, its mathematical elegance led the world's foremost expert in the neurobiological correlates of consciousness, Christof Koch to report a dramatic shift in perspective. Consciousness, he now believes, is not limited to brains and biology; it is a basic property of the information underpinning the physical world.

> 'The entire cosmos is suffused with sentience. We are surrounded and immersed in consciousness; it is in the air we breathe, the soil we tread on, the bacteria that colonize our intestines, and the brain that enables us to think.'[3]

Beginning with the discoveries of Edwin Hubble, the last century saw a dramatic expansion of our cosmology. In their seeking an understanding of this incomprehensibly vast new universe with its billions of galaxies, scientists began focusing on the universal laws guiding cosmic evolution. The values of these laws, they learned, could have coalesced within multiples of trillions of intelligible arrangements, yet only an infinitesimal number could have supported the development of complex life of any kind. Against all the odds, the constants of nature had settled in astonishing balance to create a universe fertile for life and mind. In light of such a 'coincidence', it has become parsimonious to consider a meaningful relationship between life and the larger cosmic process. Today many scientists hold space for the possibility that life and mind were in some way woven into the natural order from the beginning; that their activities somehow bring closure to a mysterious metaphysical value condition. On this new view of the universe, Davies remarks,

> '... in which the emergence of life and consciousness is seen, not as a freak set of events, but fundamental to its law-like workings, is a universe that can truly be called our home.'[4]

The 20th century also saw the field of psi research approach maturity as an empirical science. Just as modern chemistry evolved from the murky origins of medieval alchemy, psi research is the intellectual progeny of earlier, cruder 'psychical' research of the late 19th century concerned with the scientific investigation of the occult. This controversial field had been primarily initiated to investigate, among other strange phenomena, claims surrounding spiritual mediumship. In this practice, the popularity of which was then sweeping Europe and North America, individuals claimed direct psychic communication with the dead. Looking back, the evidence of that time is inconclusive, punctuated by instances of outright fraud on the part of mediums and their handlers, and times when the enthusiasm of investigators clouded their judgment. Moving into the 20th century, in their emerging field, parapsychologists increasingly abandoned the séance room, refining their study to a more scientific exploration of the relationship between mind and world. As these efforts made their way into the laboratory, this curious field found itself uniquely situated to empirically investigate the place of consciousness in nature. Clinical experiments revealed compelling evidence that mind was indeed continuous with the world. Despite the field's strange origins, thinkers in a range of scientific disciplines began recognizing the importance of questions raised by psi research. Today the scientists carrying out these investigations are no longer parapsychologists in the traditional sense; they are anthropologists, biologists, physicians, physicists and psychologists. Their evidence, for those willing to confront it, seems explicable only within a view of nature in which mind plays a fundamental role. While the field remains shrouded in controversy, over the last fifty years clinical laboratory studies have produced compelling evidence that we are not isolated beings and that our sensitivities and agency extend beyond our bodies in still mysterious ways. As the pioneer in this field, Dean Radin writes,

> 'The newly developing worldview suggests that it is no longer tenable to imagine that the universe is a mindless clockwork mechanism. Something else seems to be going on, something involving the mind and consciousness in important ways.'[5]

There now appears to be compelling scientific validation of those often-fleeting experiences of expanded interconnectedness so many have reported throughout the ages. Might episodes of transcendence, sought over millennia through a spectrum of cultural practice and ritual, have a real, veridical dimension – providing access to an expanded scope of perspective? If the mind reflects something intrinsic about the way nature is organized, perhaps it is possible to inwardly glimpse its deeper character.

THE TRANSPERSONAL SELF

For millennia people from every culture have reported mystical experiences – apparent glimpses of a profound and numinous reality lying just beyond the veil of ordinary waking consciousness. We have long had pause to question the nature of these experiences that are, at least subjectively, powerfully meaningful. Be they induced by meditation, fasting, ritual practices such as drumming or chanting, the consumption of psychedelic compounds or controlled breathing exercises, throughout history transpersonal experiences have been catalysts for creativity and, for those that encounter them, are almost invariably life changing. Individuals and their groups have undergone extraordinary hardships in pursuit of them. Buddhist monks, living deep in the Himalayas, are known to leave the sanctuary of the monastery, adopting lives of meditative solitude, sometimes taking residence in remote mountain caves. In pursuit of enlightenment, this extreme life-style is dedicated to the cultivation of episodes of transcendence: a perceived inner alignment with the ultimate nature of being. Some will live this existence for decades, but are their reported experiences of oceanic oneness and cosmic totality any more than simply a product of brain chemistry? Modern psychology and psychotherapy draw no distinction between mystical experiences and psychotic episodes, but is it possible that these states reveal something more than the architecture of the human psyche? There's no doubt that the forms of these experiences are shaped by the beliefs of the individual and their unique cultural milieu. How we might separate the structure of the human psyche, its symbols, beliefs, personal history and cultural images from anything truly representative of the larger reality is, admittedly, an extremely difficult issue. With this in view, there are some compelling similarities between those deep-felt convictions attained through contemplative practice and the emerging description of nature coalescing within the intrinsic consciousness movement. The Vedic pronouncement, 'Atman equals Brahman' is the insight that the ultimate universal reality (Brahman) is one and the same with the experiential center underlying the self (Atman). In traditions of the East, attainment of this insight is considered to be among the most fundamental of contemplative revelations. A belief in the universal nature of mind is a core tenet of Mahāyāna Buddhism, the largest tradition of Buddhism in the world today. The intrinsic nature of consciousness is not an arbitrary fact about their world picture; it deeply informs their basic practice. Taking the view that all beings are extensions of a singular pervasive principle of awareness, the resulting practice endeavors toward breaking down the perceived separation between self and other, and as a consequence is grounded in peace, compassion and non-violence. Enlightenment – the ultimate recognition of the fundamental unity of all beings and all existence, is pursued, not in service to the individual self, but for the good of all sentient beings. The concomitant belief in the full sentience of animals and a concern for their suffering further compels many Buddhists to vegetarianism. Of course, other distinct metaphysical beliefs inform their values, such as the laws of *Karma* and *rebirth*, and these closely relate to secondary beliefs about the role of conscious minds in the larger cosmic process. However, the primary belief in an intrinsic mental aspect of nature speaks directly to the core values of many contemplative traditions, and in an apparently logical, non-arbitrary way. In a coming section we will explore how the way a culture locates consciousness in its larger picture of reality, be it intrinsic, incidental, or illusory, is key to understanding its core values.

Several thinkers have observed that modern science — especially physics, is approaching a similarly holistic and interconnected view of nature to that described by Eastern traditions. Is it possible that the inner approach of the mystic and the outer approach of the physicist are two paths, destined to converge on the same essential understanding of reality? This was a view perhaps most famously argued by the physicist Fritjof Capra in his 1975 best seller, *The Tao of Physics*.[6] He highlighted many compelling parallels between the insights of enlightened sages and the new reality hailed by modern physics. Is it possible that committed contemplative practice led these spiritual seekers to experience something more veridical and primary than their sense impressions? If a post-materialist science is destined to recognize human consciousness as an aspect of nature's evolving interiority, consciousness itself could become an instrument of scientific study. Perhaps, as the physicist and Buddhist scholar B. Allan Wallace suggests, such first-person methods will involve the development of refined contemplative states that may not be altogether dissimilar to those developed in contemplative traditions.[7] It may turn out, he argues, that only through a deeper phenomenological study based on direct experience can we probe the intrinsic inner nature of the world.

In the cultural lore of traditions revering mystical and transpersonal experiences, these states are often accompanied by reports of psychic episodes. While the more dramatic of these accounts may be attributable to historical embellishment and story telling, modern experiments indicate to the psi-conducive nature of altered and contemplative states. The evidence suggests that these experiences may indeed have a transpersonal dimension; exceeding the usually accepted limits of the mind. Whatever our response to this evidence, if consciousness is intrinsic to physics, as many scientists and philosophers now argue, I think we should hold space for the possibility that those long-revered practices of diving inward can also be a source of insight about reality.

DISPUTED TERRITORY

While today there is growing recognition that consciousness represents a real feature on the metaphysical landscape, there are many scientists and educated thinkers that sharply disagree. Many view themselves as defending the sacred scientific process from the corrupting influence of magical thinking. Their noble aim is to banish superstitious and irrational beliefs. But in their haste to enlighten the masses and dispel any mystery from which superstition might foam, many have proven willing to deny the existence of their own subjective experience, deflating consciousness to an illusion.

This often leads to their ignorance, dismissal or excessive skeptical prejudice toward any evidence that consciousness is something more. The most vocal critics identify proudly as rational atheists, and quite apart from the ordinary activities of science, are engaged in an on-going culture war with religion. In this conflict, consciousness is a territory that must be captured and neutralized of any deeper significance. The problem, however, is that consciousness is more than a poorly understood area of the natural world that has been wrongfully appropriated to superstitious beliefs; it is the basis of all value and meaning. It is ground zero in humanity's search to understand its place in the universe. In light of these stakes, it is difficult to justify some academics' eagerness to pave over the mystery of consciousness. In such cases, the drive to sanitize mind of any ontological or metaphysical significance is often, in essence, ideological.

Aspects of the emerging consciousness-involving view of our universe are not inconsistent with attributes the religiously inclined may comfortably ascribe to 'God.' As physicist Freeman Dyson wrote in his book, *Infinite In All Directions*,

> 'If we believe in this mental component of the universe, then we can say that we are small pieces of God's mental apparatus.'[8]

We will always be free to call the universe or the total order of existence 'God', and many scientists and philosophers have chosen to do so, if only as a metaphor. An issue is that the meaning of this word seems often to differ as much between individuals as it does between cultures. Recognizing the existence of an indwelling creative impulse may satisfy the criteria for some people's definition of god, and yet it may lack critical characteristics of others. Given how heavily overburdened the word 'God' can quickly become, I find myself trying to avoid it. Religious traditions have developed what are for many people, indispensible practices for the expansion of consciousness and the cultivation of experiences of a larger reality, but I am cautious of appropriating our ever-evolving view of nature with any particular human religion or conception of the divine. While religious belief may be a product of the correct intuition – that all life has inherent meaning in a larger context – there is no convincing evidence, at least that I am aware of, for why any one or amalgamation of existing religious doctrines should contain the full story of our place in the universe. In view of these reservations, I think an understanding of the universe that intrinsically involves the evolution of life and consciousness will have profound implications for us, some of which may appropriately be termed 'spiritual'. We'll explore some of these in the final section of this book.

THE EVOLUTION OF CONSCIOUSNESS

A general view among many thinkers of the intrinsic consciousness movement is that science and philosophy's emerging description of the world no longer marginalizes deeper views of consciousness; it *calls* for them. Our mistake, they argue, has been to anthropomorphize consciousness, as if it were a biological oddity or fluke of natural selection. In our desire to bravely confront humanity's ever more decentralized place in the universe, we have arguably committed the most hubristic example of human exceptionalism yet. By appropriating all mind, meaning and value to ourselves, we summarily justified dispensing with them as mere human categories. The great irony, as cultural historian Richard Tarnas observes, is that,

> '...just when the modern mind believes it has most fully purified itself from any anthropomorphic projections, when it actively construes the world as unconscious, mechanistic, and impersonal, it is just then that the world is most completely a selective construct of the human mind.'[9]

The view that judged the universe as dead, inert, and unconscious, also failed to locate consciousness in those very minds that conceived it. While it describes a world that is essentially value-free, it can also be seen to promote decidedly bleak, even destructive values. Fritjof Capra once called this the 'crisis of perception.'[10] Seeing ourselves as essentially separate from other people, separate from other nations, and separate from Earth and its living biosphere, all contribute to an ethical posture that is strained to encompass anything broader than the local self and its immediate environment. Many thinkers have considered that the current social and environmental crises have their roots in a disenchanted worldview that cuts consciousness out of the world and with it any intrinsic value or meaning. In his book *Panpsychism in the West*, the philosopher David Skrbina provides a lucid survey of the history and recent resurgence of deeper views of consciousness in Western philosophy.[11] In his conclusions he considers how the estrangement of consciousness from our picture of nature has wrought consequences far beyond science and philosophy. It has radically informed society's overall world-view, deeply imbedded itself within our collective psyche, and become reflected in our most basic values. Our selfish individualism, the unsustainable exploitation of the environment and other species, and the lack of concern for unborn future generations, may all be symptomatic of an isolating and fragmented worldview in which the self is finite and profoundly alone in its meaning – fundamentally separate from the world and other beings. Scientific materialism, in its failure to honor life and mind's place in the world, has led to a runaway reductionism, where the mind is 'nothing but' the brain, life is 'nothing but' biological machinery, and the universe is 'nothing but' a freak energy event in an infinite vacuum of nothing. As Skrbina reflects,

> 'The mechanistic worldview once liberated humanity from religious dogma. Now, some would say, it has outlived its usefulness. It has become its own dogma, more stifling and destructive than the one it usurped.'[12]

Philosophical systems that take an intrinsic perspective toward consciousness, on the other hand, embrace the indispensible findings of science, yet avoid the critical error of psychophysical reductionism. They point toward a compelling middle way that, in addition to the merit in succeeding where other views have failed in uniting mind and world, also carry the attractive aesthetic of cultivating a more life-affirming matrix of values that is both constructive and unifying. Life's interior dimension is no longer seen as an insignificant illusion, but an ontological reality, embedded in and continuous with the larger cosmic order. In this more primary identity – as the universe seeking itself into being through form, the boundaries between 'other' and 'self' are more porous, allowing for greater sensitivity and intimacy with the world and other beings, and ultimately a view with greater scope for compassion, care, and cooperation. Skrbina refers to the attractive aesthetic values of deeper views of self as the 'greater virtue argument' – that intrinsic views of consciousness inherently seem to promote positive, sustaining and more harmonious values.[13] Might this harmony be a result of their reflecting a better approximation of the true nature of things? –Simply a better basic model of reality for us to attune? Among more open-minded scientists and philosophers it is becoming increasingly apparent that the expanded conception of identity hailed by deeper views of consciousness is not only required for a satisfactory philosophical account of the mental, it may also be essential for our realizing the critical values needed to respond to the looming social, geopolitical and environmental cataclysms that face us.

Consciousness is the ground of all value and meaning in the universe. Significance exists only within its occasion and creation in consciousness. If the universe is at all a meaningful place, it will be so because consciousness plays an intrinsic role in its evolution. But could we ever identify principles guiding the evolution of consciousness, wherever it emerges in the universe? –True in every instance of life? Such an understanding could provide for an 'objective' basis of values, and perhaps even the possibility of a form of universal morality. I suspect that it may indeed be possible, even without a full understanding of mind's relationship to the rest of reality. While minds may differ vastly in their contents and organization, in their development toward greater valency of capacity and complexity, they are all subject to the same spatiotemporal conditions of all other life in the known universe. Indeed, if we speak broadly, amid life's rich diversity, consciousness is evolving in characteristic ways.

In all cases societies of minds evolve together through cooperation. It makes an almost cold economic sense for minds to pool their cognitive resources, wherever possible, to make better decisions. As species advance in complexity, such economies of insight will naturally emerge. The mind's capacity for cooperation advances in step with its capacity to identify with the goals and intentions of other minds. In us, this involves the cultivation of boundary-dissolving and binding emotions, such as those we identify as empathy, love and compassion. While humans have proven very creative in their development of weapons and means of oppression, when orientated toward the basic value of lifting consciousness, it will always be preferable to cultivate rather than stifle creativity. Similarly, cooperation will always be preferable to conflict, compassion will always be preferable to cruelty, and knowledge will always be preferable to ignorance. None of these values are characteristically human; instead they pertain, as all values necessarily do, to consciousness and its evolution. The cosmos may be inhabited by minds belonging to a vast diversity of beings, and yet the moral and ethical principles toward which their cultures tend may well be surprisingly similar. Once a society of minds recognizes its shared collective identity, selfishness, slavery and the suppression of others are simply no longer viable survival modes. They are therefore increasingly unlikely to be operating in more advanced cultures. It could be a natural trend that maturing civilizations come to recognize their collective identity by the fact of their consciousness, and thus recognize 'self' within all conscious beings they encounter. If we have intelligent galactic neighbors, it is not only highly likely that we could comprehend and empathize with their inner mental life, our meeting, if we deem one another ready, would compel us into a shared and expanding economy of insight.

TECHNOLOGY AND CONSCIOUSNESS

As modern technologies continue to dramatically change human life, for better or worse, we are also gaining the ability to change ourselves. Whether we embrace these new technologies or fear them, there seems to be no halting their advance. We are now glimpsing the means to change not only our physical expressions, but also our cognitive architecture and emotional responses. How should we regard the use of these technologies? —As misguided departures from Mother Nature's guiding hands, or extensions of the ongoing creative evolution of life and mind?

It is an open question whether consciousness can be instantiated in an artificial substrate, but if the mental and the physical are truly continuous, why should an appropriately organized system not also be conscious? The brain is the most complex structure we know of, but equally there doesn't seem to be anything 'special' about brain matter that fundamentally distinguishes it from all other matter. I suspect it may indeed be possible to create a conscious artificial system, and yet minds like ours could turn out to be much more complex than we anticipate. A general misunderstanding about the nature of consciousness may also present an obstruction toward the creation of conscious artificial intelligence. On the other hand it also seems possible that we might eventually create a conscious system that draws from an advanced understanding of the processes and organization of the brain and yet we may initially fail to recognize that the consciousness expressed by the system is not created within it, but instead reflects and modulates an intrinsic perspectival character of reality itself. It is also an open question if such technologies already exist. The neuroscientist Christof Koch has speculated that the internet, which comprises some 10 million computers and 10 times more participating transistors than there are synapses in the human brain, might contain the first glimmerings of awareness.[14] At this stage we can only speculate about the potentials of conscious AI. The dawning of artificial intelligence, conscious or otherwise, will have far reaching implications to human life, the Earth, and possibly the future of all conscious life in the universe. Whether or not conscious AI is possible in the foreseeable future, technologies allowing us to augment our cognitive architecture may come much sooner. We already live in a world in which technologically facilitated brain-to-brain communication is a reality, and thoughts (or at least their electrocortical correlates) can dialogue via the internet with a remote computer interface. With such technologies come challenging new questions about human nature and the values that guide us. What will be the implications for our concepts of human nature if, say by neural implant or genetic engineering, it becomes possible to safely enhance compassionate and altruistic emotions while suppressing those also all-too-human violent and retributive ones? As we take our evolution into our own hands the values that guide us will no longer be specifically human. If we can navigate the social consequences of our burgeoning technology, and survive the various challenges that pose a threat to our survival, ultimately I think our values are destined to converge on that which defines us: our consciousness. While any understanding of the principles guiding conscious evolution will itself be continually evolving, there is ultimately no moral issue that does not finally reduce to a concern about consciousness and its evolution. If it is capable of surviving its vulnerable adolescence, perhaps this, in due time, will be recognized by any sufficiently advanced society of minds.

THE RE-ENCHANTMENT OF THE COSMOS

The potential for meaning in our larger cosmological perspective ultimately depends on what we understand consciousness to be. If it is real – *really* real, then value and meaning become existing and necessary features of the universe. Between the life denying ethic of reductive materialism, and the blind faith of religious fundamentalism, the emerging perspective offers a middle path: a view of the world that accommodates both our scientific knowledge as well as embracing the traditionally religious intuition – that we play a meaningful role in the larger cosmic scheme of things. This emerging view is accompanied by the dawning realization that neither the organism nor the universe is akin to a machine. A machine, after all, is a human-made object, found nowhere in nature but of our own creation. Indeed, the universe increasingly seems to exhibit more of the characteristics of a living, evolving organism than it does an inert mechanism. The machine metaphor of our universe, as biologist Rupert Sheldrake writes,

> '... has long outlived its usefulness, and holds back scientific thinking in physics, biology and medicine. Our evolving universe is an organism, and so is the earth, and so are oak trees, and so are dogs, and so are you.' [15]

The developing image of nature is not of a compendium of particles and molecules blindly subservient to physical and chemical laws; it is an evolving, vital, and creative process. The philosopher Theo Badashi has offered the term 'cosmohumanism' to describe the dawning perspective in which life is understood '... not as a random 'accident' but as a function of the Earth's and universe's own evolutionary processes.'[16] This emerging view profoundly resituates us from an isolating reductive view of life and mind, finding us in a universe that is once again alive to us. Instead of helpless spectators of a meaningless explosion gradually fading into darkness, we can see ourselves as active participators in a great unfoldment of cosmic creativity – a universe still in the process of creation. As we begin to recognize the limits of materialism and the larger reality beckoning beyond, there is the sense of waking, as if from a dream, to find our self in a re-enchanted universe in which we truly belong. The human being may not be the center of this universe, and yet the rise of conscious life more generally seems mysteriously woven into the cosmic code. Life finds itself invested into a larger evolving matrix of meaning that appears inextricably linked to the integrity of the entire system.

In this book I have introduced the 'intrinsic consciousness movement' to describe the modest rise in popularity of views that, in full acceptance of the discovered facts of science, locates consciousness, or the inherent potential for it, intrinsically to the foundations of nature. Today a constellation of respected academics now regards the flowering of life and mind, not as arbitrary or 'accidental', but as an essential unfolding in the cycle of existence. If we can achieve a more open-minded science, the psi evidence, previously rejected or ignored, has the potential to revolutionize our understanding of our situation in being. Perhaps most pertinently to science, it offers an empirical if indirect means of probing the subtle relationships between mind and world, while at the same time serving as a catalyzing reminder of our deeper nature. The view that recognizes the inner nature of our minds as an extension of the intrinsic interior dimension of the universe describes minds as truly continuous with the world and with each other. If we define our fundamental identity, not as our thoughts and personal stories, but as that irreducible consciousness which experiences them, then at the core of who we are, we share in a single unified self that transcends and includes all conscious beings. This is what the psi evidence suggests – that within this more primary self we are deeply and meaningfully connected. The picture emerging from the frontiers of modern thought asserts that truly, we are not separate. The age-old saying, 'we are one' is more than a rallying cry for hippies and New Age enthusiasts, it turns out to be a fundamental truth of our most basic nature. Reality is a much more mysterious place than many of us suspected, and a new open-mindedness will be necessary for our understanding to progress. There is no way to foresee the language or models that will prove basic to our future envisioning of the universe, and yet it increasingly seems that consciousness will be an indispensable concept. Through the theories and evidence of a range of disciplines we have explored the possibility that beyond the bleak and ailing outlook of reductive materialism a more meaningful view of life and consciousness is possible. Real meaning in our universe is not contingent on the accuracy of our religious texts, nor is the cosmic vastness surrounding us an indicator of life's insignificance. The story given to us by our modern seeking can be a spiritual one, in the respect that it can be the source of a sense of awe, meaning, interconnectedness and even greater purpose. If we are willing to open ourselves to the ideas and evidence, there are already compelling reasons to consider conscious beings such as we are intimately at home in the universe.

REFERENCES

Jung, C.G. (1959). *The archetypes and the collective unconscious.* Princeton, NJ: Princeton University Press. (p. 270).

Chapter 1. THE QUESTION OF CONSCIOUSNESS

1. Putnam, H. (1960). Minds and machines. In S. Hook (Ed.), *Dimensions of Mind* (pp. 57-80). NY, New York: New York University Press.
2. Nagel, T. (1974). What is it like to be a bat?. *The Philosophical Review, 83*(4), 435-50.
3. Chalmers, D. J. (1995). Facing up to the problem of consciousness. *Journal of Consciousness Studies, 2*(3), 200-219.
4. Baum, W. M. (1994). *Understanding behaviorism: Science, behavior, and culture.* New York, NY: HarperCollins College Publishers.
5. Koch, C. (2012). *Consciousness: Confessions of a romantic reductionist.* Cambridge, MA: MIT press.
6. Levine, J. (1983). Materialism and qualia: The explanatory gap. *Pacific Philosophical Quarterly, 64*(4), 354-361.
7. Damasio, A. (2002). How the brain creates the mind. Scientific American - The Hidden Mind.
8. Descartes, R. (1641). *Meditations on First Philosophy.* (J. Cottingham & B. Williams, Trans.). Cambridge, UK: Cambridge University Press.

9. Chalmers, D. J. (1997). *The conscious mind: In search of a fundamental theory.* Oxford, NY: Oxford University Press.

10. Jackson F. (1986). Comments and criticism: What Mary didn't know. *The Journal of Philosophy, 83*(5), 291-295.

11. Dennett, D. C. (1988). Quining Qualia. In A. J. Marcel & E. Bisiach (Eds.), *Consciousness in Contemporary Science.* Oxford, UK: Oxford University Press.

12. Harris, S. (2014). *Waking Up: A Guide to Spirituality Without Religion.* Simon and Schuster. (p. 53).

13. Nagel, T. (1979). Panpsychism. In *Mortal Questions.* (pp. 181-196). New York, NY: Cambridge University Press.

14. Chalmers, D. J. (2002). *The puzzle of conscious experience. Scientific American - The Hidden Mind.* (pp. 90-100).

15. Chalmers, D. (2014). *David Chalmers: How do you explain consciousness?* [Video file]. Retrieved from http://www.ted.com

16. Low, P., Panksepp, J., Reiss, D., Edelman, D., Van Swinderen, B., & Koch, C. (2012). *The Cambridge declaration on consciousness.*

17. As cited in: Ehrenwald, J. (1978). Einstein Skeptical of ESP? Postscript to a correspondence. *Journal of Parapsychology, 42,* 137-142.

18. James, W. (1890). *The principles of psychology.* New York: H. Holt and Company. (p.149)

Chapter 2. THE INNER LANDSCAPE

1. Skrbina, D. (2005). *Panpsychism in the West.* Cambridge, MA: MIT Press Books. (p. 3)
2. Russell, B. (1956). *Portraits from memory: And other essays.* London, UK: Allen & Unwin. (p.153)
3. As cited in Seager, W. (2005). Panpsychism. *Encyclopedia of Cognitive Science.*
4. De Chardin, P. T. (1999). *The human phenomenon.* (S. Appleton-Weber, Trans.). Sussex, UK: Sussex Academic Press.
5. Eddington, A. (1920). *Space, Time and Gravitation: An Outline of the General Relativity Theory.* Cambridge, UK: Cambridge University Press. (p.200)
6. Goff, P. (25 May 2014). How Come Consciousness? *Philosophy Now Radio Show #36 Podcast.* Podcast retrieved from: https://philosophynow.org
7. Nagel, T. (2012). *Mind and cosmos: Why the materialist neo-Darwinian conception of nature is almost certainly false.* New York, NY: Oxford University Press.
8. Tononi, G. (2008). Consciousness as integrated information: A provisional manifesto. *The Biological Bulletin, 215*(3), 216-242.
9. Tononi, G. (2007). *Guilio Tononi: Consciousness and the brain* [Video file]. Retrieved from http://vimeo.com/53787308
10. Koch, C. (2014, January 1). Is consciousness universal? *Scientific American.*

11. Zimmer, C. (2010, September 20). Sizing up consciousness by its bits. *The New York Times*
12. Pagel, P. (2012, 01 August). How to measure consciousness. *New Scientist.*
13. Koch, C. (2014, January 1). Is consciousness universal? *Scientific American.*
14. Massimini, M., Ferrarelli, F., Huber, R., Esser, S. K., Singh, H., & Tononi, G. (2005). Breakdown of cortical effective connectivity during sleep. *Science, 309*(5744), 2228-2232.
15. Sperry, R. W. (1968). Hemisphere deconnection and unity in conscious awareness. *American Psychologist, 23*(10), 723-733.
16. Koch, C. (2012). *Consciousness: Confessions of a Romantic Reductionist.* Cambridge, MA: MIT Press Books.
17. Wheeler, J. A. (1990). Information, physics, quantum: The search for links. In W. Zurek (Ed.), *Complexity, Entropy, and the Physics of Information.* Redwood City. CA: Addison-Wesley.
18. Chalmers, D. J. (1995). Facing up to the hard problem of consciousness, *Journal of Consciousness Studies 2*(3), 200-219.
19. As cited in Pais, A. (2000). *The genius of science: A portrait gallery.* Oxford, UK: Oxford University Press.
20. Engel, G. S., Calhoun, T. R., Read, E. L., Ahn, T. K., Mančal, T., Cheng, Y. C., ... & Fleming, G. R. (2007). Evidence for wavelike energy transfer through quantum coherence in photosynthetic systems. *Nature, 446*(7137), 782-786.

21. Maeda, K., Henbest, K. B., Cintolesi, F., Kuprov, I., Rodgers, C. T., Liddell, P., ... & Hore, P. J. (2008). Chemical compass model of avian magnetoreception. *Nature, 453*(7193), 387–390.

22. Lloyd, S. (2011). Quantum coherence in biological systems. *Journal of Physics: Conference Series, 302*(1).

23. Ball, P. (2011). The dawn of quantum biology. *Nature, 474*(7351), 272-274.

24. Heisenberg, W. (1971) *Physics and beyond*. Cambridge, University Press, (p.101)

25. Hameroff, S., & Penrose, R. (1996). Orchestrated reduction of quantum coherence in brain microtubules: A model for consciousness. *Mathematics and computers in simulation, 40*(3), 453-480.

26. Ghosh, S., Sahu, S., & Bandyopadhyay, A. (2014). Evidence of massive global synchronization and the consciousness: Comment on "Consciousness in the universe: A review of the 'Orch OR' theory" by Hameroff and Penrose. *Physics of Life Reviews 83*(4), 94-100.

27. Planck, M. (1993). *A survey of physical theory*. (R. Jones & D. H. Williams, Trans.). New York, NY: Dover Publications, Inc.

Chapter 3. MIND AND MATTER

1. Planck, M. (1931, January 25). *The Observer*, London, UK
2. Wigner, E. P. (1961). Remarks on the Mind-Body Question. In Wheeler J. A., & Zurek, W. H. (Eds.), (1984), *Quantum theory and measurement.* (pp.168-181). Princeton, NJ: Princeton University Press. (p.169)
3. Schrödinger, E. (1931, January 25). *The Observer*, London, UK.
4. Jammer, M. (1974). *The philosophy of quantum mechanics: Interpretations of quantum mechanics in historical perspectives.* New York, NY: Wiley Interscience. (p. 151)
5. Von Neumann, J. (1955). *Mathematical foundations of quantum mechanics.* Princeton, NJ: Princeton University Press.
6. Pietikainen, P. (2002). *Atom and archetype. The Pauli/Jung letters, 1932-1958,.* Princeton, NJ: Princeton University Press.
7. Rosenblum, B., & Kuttner, F. (2006). *Quantum Enigma: Physics encounters consciousness.* New York, NY: Oxford University Press.
8. Arndt, M., Nairz, O., Vos-Andreae, J., Keller, C., Van der Zouw, G., & Zeilinger, A. (1999). Wave–particle duality of C60 molecules. *Nature, 401*(6754), 680-682.
9. Rosenblum, B., & Kuttner, F. (2006). *Quantum Enigma: Physics encounters consciousness.* New York, NY: Oxford University Press.
10. Quoted by Jammer, M. (1974). *The philosophy of quantum mechanics: The interpretations of quantum mechanics in historical perspectives.* New York, NY: John Wiley & Sons, Inc. (p. 151)

11. Planck, M. (1932). *Where is science going?*. (J. V. Murphy, Trans.). New York, NY: W. W. Norton & Company, Inc.

12. Feynman, R. P. (1967). *The character of physical law*. (Vol. 66). Cambridge, MA: MIT press.

13. Davies, P. (2006). *The Goldilocks enigma: Why is the universe just right for life?*. London, UK: Penguin Books Ltd.

14. d'Espagnat, B. (1979). The quantum theory and reality. *Scientific American, 241*(5), 158-181.

15. Dyson, F. J. (1979). *Disturbing the universe*. New York, NY: Harper & Row.

16. Penrose, R. (1999). *The emperor's new mind: Concerning computers, minds, and the laws of physics*. Oxford, UK: Oxford University Press.

17. Stapp H.P. (2007). *Mindful universe: Quantum mechanics and the participating observer*. Heidelberg, BW: Springer-Verlag.

18. Linde, A. (2003). Inflation, quantum cosmology and the anthropic principle. In J. D. Barrow, P. C. W. Davies & C. L. Harper Jr (Eds.), *Science and Ultimate Reality: Quantum Theory, Cosmology, and Complexity* (426-458). Cambridge, UK: Cambridge University Press.

19. Stapp, H. P. (2007). Quantum approaches to consciousness. In P. D. Zelazo, M. Moscovitch & E. Thompson (Eds.), *Cambridge Handbook of Consciousness* (p.881-908). New York, NY: Cambridge University Press.

20. Chalmers, D. J. (2010). *The character of consciousness*. New York, NY: Oxford University Press. (p.128)

21. Chalmers, D. J. Consciousness and the collapse of the wave function [Video file]. Retrieved from: https://www.youtube.com/watch?v=DIBT6E2GtjA
22. d'Espagnat, B. (1979). The quantum theory and reality. *Scientific American, 241*(5), 158-181.

Chapter 4. ANOMALOUS OBSERVATIONS

1. Radin, D. I. (2008). Testing nonlocal observation as a source of intuitive knowledge. *Explore: The Journal of Science and Healing, 4*(1), 25-35.
2. Radin, D. I. Entangled minds and beyond [Video file]. Retrieved from: https://www.youtube.com/watch?v=kKuwWBYHQ50
3. Radin, D. I. (2008). Testing nonlocal observation as a source of intuitive knowledge. *Explore: The Journal of Science and Healing, 4*(1), 25-35.
4. Radin, D. I., Michel, L., Galdamez, K., Wendland, P., Rickenbach, R., & Delorme, A. (2012). Consciousness and the double-slit interference pattern: Six experiments. *Physics Essays, 25*(2), 157-171.
5. Radin, D. (2013). *Supernormal: Science, yoga, and the evidence for extraordinary psychic abilities.* New York, NY: Random House, Inc. (p. 243)
6. Ibid.

7. Wheeler, J. A. (1983). Law without law. In J. A. Wheeler & W. H. Zurek (Eds.), *Quantum theory and measurement* (182-213). Princeton, NJ: Princeton University Press. (p. 192)
8. Radin, D., Michel, L., Johnston, J., & Delorme, A., (2013). Psychophysical interactions with a double-slit interference pattern. *Physics Essays, 26*(4), 553-566.

Chapter 5. CONSCIOUSNESS AS AN ORDERING PRINCIPLE

1. Rhine, J. B. (1971). *Progress in Parapsychology.* Durham, NC: Parapsychology Press.
2. Schmidt, H. (1993). Observation of a psychokinetic effect under highly controlled conditions. *Journal of Parapsychology, 57*(4), 351-72.
3. Dunne, B. J., & Jahn, R. G. (2005). The PEAR Proposition. *Journal of Scientific Exploration, 19*(2), 195–245.
4. Ibid.
5. Dunne, B. J., & Jahn, R. G. (1992). Experiments in remote human/machine interaction. *Journal of Scientific Exploration, 6*(4), 311-332.
6. Tressoldi, P., Pederzoli, L., Caini, P., Ferrini, A., Melloni, S., Richeldi, D., ... & Duma, G. M. (2014). Mind-Matter interaction at a distance of 190 km: Effects on a random event generator using a cutoff method. *NeuroQuantology, 12*(3), 337-343.

7. Dunne, B. J., & Jahn, R. G. (1992). Experiment in remote human/machine interaction. *Journal of Scientific Exploration, 6*(4), 311–332.
8. Schmidt, H. (1969). Precognition of a quantum process. *Journal of Parapsychology, 33*(2), 99–108.
9. Nelson, R. D., Bradish, G. J., Dobyns, Y. H., Dunne, B. J., & Jahn, R. G. (1996). FieldREG anomalies in group situations. *Journal of Scientific Exploration, 10*(1), 111-141.
10. De Chardin, P. T. (1964). *The future of man.* (N. Denny, Trans.). New York, NY: Harper & Row.
11. Nelson, R. (2006). The Global Consciousness Project. *EXPLORE: The Journal of Science and Healing, 2*(4), 342-351.
12. Radin, D. I. (2006). *Entangled Minds: Extrasensory experiences in quantum reality.* New York, NY: Simon & Schuster. (p.200)
13. Radin, D. I. (2002). Exploring relationships between random physical events and mass human attention: Asking for whom the bell tolls. *Journal of Scientific Exploration, 16*(4), 533-547.
14. Radin, D. I. (2001). Global Consciousness Project: Analysis for September 11, 2001.
15. Radin, D. I., Vieten, C., Burnett, J., Delorme, A., & Hunt, T. (2013). *Deviations from Randomness Associated with Collective Attention: Burning Man 2012*
16. Ibid.

17. On Noetic Science: Cassandra Vieten at TEDxBlackRockCity [Video file]. Retrieved from:

    https://www.youtube.com/watch?v=FoCABSb9KP0

18. *Research into Collective Consciousness at Burning Man* (2012 & 2013).

19. Ibid.

20. Quote by Radin, D. I. Beyond entangled minds [Video file]. Retrieved from:

    https://www.youtube.com/watch?v=kKuwWBYHQ50

21. Ibid.

22. Ibid.

23. Turing, A. M. (1950). Computing machinery and intelligence. *Mind*, 59(236) 433-460.

Chapter 6. ENTANGLED PERCEPTIONS

1. Tart, C. T. (1963). Physiological correlates of psi cognition. *International Journal of* Parapsychology, 5, 375-386.

2. Duane T. D., & Behrendt, T. (1965). *Extrasensory electroencephalographic induction between identical twins. Science, 150*(3694), 367.

3. Targ, R., & Puthoff, H. (1974). Information transmission under conditions of sensory shielding. *Nature, 251*(5476), 602-607.

4. Wackermann, J., Seiter, C., Keibel, H., & Walach, H. (2003). Correlations between brain electrical activities of two spatially separated human subjects. *Neuroscience Letters, 336*(1), 60-64.

5. Standish, L. J., Kozak, L., Johnson L. C., & Richards, T. (2004). Electroencephalographic evidence of correlated event-related signals between the brains of spatially and sensory isolated human subjects. *The Journal of Alternative and Complementary Medicine, 10*(2), 307-314.
6. Radin, D. I. (2004). Event-related electroencephalographic correlations between isolated human subjects. *The Journal of Alternative & Complementary Medicine, 10*(2), 315-323.

Chapter 7. SHARING INNER SPACE

1. Ullman, M., Krippner, S., & Vaughan, A. (1989). *Dream telepathy: Experiments in nocturnal ESP* (2nd ed.). Jefferson, NC: McFarland.
2. Radin, D. I. (2006). *Entangled Minds: Extrasensory experiences in quantum reality*. New York, NY: Simon & Schuster. (p. 120)
3. Bem, D. J. (1996). Ganzfeld phenomena. In G. Stein (Ed.), *Encyclopaedia of the paranormal* (pp. 291-296). Buffalo, NY: Prometheus Books.
4. Ibid.
5. Hyman, R. (1991). [Replication and Meta-Analysis in Parapsychology]: Comment. *Statistical Science, 6*(4), 389-392. (p. 392)
6. Radin, D. I. (2006). *Entangled Minds: Extrasensory experiences in quantum reality*. New York, NY: Simon & Schuster. (p. 120)
7. Radin, D. I. (2006). *Entangled Minds: Extrasensory experiences in quantum reality*. New York, NY: Simon & Schuster. (p. 121)

8. Delgado-Romero, E. A., & Howard, G. S. (2005). Finding and correcting flawed research literatures. *The Humanistic Psychologist, 33*(4), 293-303. Chicago
9. Ibid.
10. Ibid.
11. Ibid.
12. Storm, L., Tressoldi, P. E., & Di Risio, L. (2010). Meta-analysis of free-response studies, 1992–2008: Assessing the noise reduction model in parapsychology. *Psychological Bulletin, 136*(4), 471–485.
13. Radin, D. I. (2006). *Entangled Minds: Extrasensory experiences in quantum reality.* New York, NY: Simon & Schuster. (p. 264)
14. D. Radin, personal communication, September 12, 2013.

Chapter 8. MIND IN TIME

1. Honorton, C., & Ferrari, D. C. (1989). Future telling: A meta-analysis of forced-choice precognition experiments, 1935–1987. *Journal of Parapsychology, 53*(28), 1-308. Retrieved from: http://www.deanradin.com
2. Radin, D. I. (1997). Unconscious perception of future emotions: An experiment in presentiment. *Journal of Scientific Exploration, 11*(2), 163-180.
3. Ibid.

4. Bierman, D. J. (2000). Anomalous baseline effects in mainstream emotion research using psychophysiological variables. *Journal of Parapsychology, 64,* 239-240.
5. Bierman, D. J., & Scholte H. S. (2002). A fMRI brain imaging study of presentiment. *Journal of International Society of Life Information Science, 20*(2), 380-388.
6. Spottiswoode S. J. P., & May E. C. (2003). Skin conductance prestimulus response: Analyses, artifacts and a pilot study. *Journal of Scientific Exploration, 17*(4), 617-641.
7. McCraty, R., Atkinson, M., & Bradley, R. T. (2004). Electrophysiological evidence of intuition: Part 2. A system-wide process? *Journal of Alternative Complementary Medicine, 10*(2), 325-336.
8. Radin, D. I., Vieten, C., Michel, L., & Delorme, A. (2011). Electrocortical activity prior to unpredictable stimuli in meditators and nonmeditators. *Explore: The Journal of Science and Healing, 7*(5), 286-299.
9. Bem, D. J. (2011). Feeling the future: experimental evidence for anomalous retroactive influences on cognition and affect. *Journal of Personality and Social Psychology, 100*(3), 407–425.
10. Ibid.
11. French, C. (2012, March 15). Precognition studies and the curse of the failed replications. *The Guardian.* London, UK.
12. Mossbridge, J., Tressoldi, P., & Utts, J. (2012). Predictive physiological anticipation preceding seemingly unpredictable stimuli: a meta-analysis. *Frontiers in Psychology, 3.*

13. Mossbridge, J. A., Tressoldi, P., Utts, J., Ives, J. A., Radin, D., & Jonas, W. B. (2014). Predicting the unpredictable: Critical analysis and practical implications of predictive anticipatory activity. *Frontiers in Human Neuroscience, 8.*

14. Bem, D., Tressoldi, P. E., Rabeyron, T., & Duggan, M. (2014). *Feeling the Future: A Meta-Analysis of 90 Experiments on the Anomalous Anticipation of Random Future Events.*

15. Dennett, D. C. (1992). Temporal anomalies of consciousness. In Y. Christen & P. S. Churchland (Eds.), *Neurophilosophy and Alzheimer's Disease* (pp. 5-17). Heidelberg, BW: Springer-Verlag.

16. Radin, D. I., Vieten, C., Michel, L., & Delorme, A. (2011). Electrocortical activity prior to unpredictable stimuli in meditators and nonmeditators. *Explore: The Journal of Science and Healing, 7*(5), 286-299.

17. Luke, D. P., Delanoy, D., & Sherwood, S. J. (2008). Psi may look like luck: Perceived luckiness and beliefs about luck in relation to precognition. *Journal of the Society for Psychical Research, 72*(4), 193-207.

18. Schmidt, H. (1976). PK effect on pre-recorded targets. *Journal of the American Society for Psychical Research, 70*(3), 267-291.

Chapter 9. THE VIEW FROM HERE

1. Radin, D. (2004). The feeling of being stared at: An analysis and replication. *Journal of the Society for Psychical Research, 68,* 246-53.

2. Braud, W. (2003). *Distant mental influence: Its contributions to science, healing, and human interactions.* Charlottesville, VA: Hampton Roads Publishing Company.
3. Sheldrake, R. (2003). *The sense of being stared at: And other aspects of the extended mind.* New York, NY: Crown Publishers.
4. Braud, W. (2003). *Distant mental influence: Its contributions to science, healing, and human interactions.* Charlottesville, VA: Hampton Roads Publishing Company.
5. Braud, W. & Schlitz, M. (1983). Psychokinetic influence on electrodermal activity. *Journal of Parapsychology, 47*(2), 95-119.
6. Kuhn, T. S. (2012). *The structure of scientific revolutions.* University of Chicago press.
7. Dyson, F. J. (1979). *Disturbing the universe.* New York, NY: Harper & Row. (p. 250)

Chapter 10. THE MEANINGFUL UNIVERSE

1. Redfern, M. (Presenter) & Deutsch, D. (Speaker). (2006, February 18). [Radio broadcast]. In P. Newman (Producer), The Anthropic Universe, The Science Show. Sydney, Australia: ABC Radio.
2. Michael Turner as quoted in Prager, D. (2013, June 18). Why some scientists embrace the multiverse. *National Review.*
3. Davies, P. (2006). *The Goldilocks Enigma: Why is the universe just right for life?.* London, UK: Penguin Books.

4. Wheeler, J. A. (1978). The "past" and the "delayed-choice" double-slit experiment. In A. R. Marlow (Ed.), *Mathematical Foundations of Quantum Theory* (pp. 9-48). New York, NY: Academic Press, Inc.
5. Manning, A. G., Khakimov, R. I., Dall, R. G., & Truscott, A. G. (2015). Wheeler's delayed-choice gedanken experiment with a single atom. *Nature Physics*.
6. Wheeler, J. A. (1983). Law without law. In J. A. Wheeler & W. H. Zurek (Eds.), *Quantum theory and measurement* (pp. 182-213). Princeton, NJ: Princeton University Press. (p. 209)
7. Wheeler, J. A. (1977). Genesis and observership. *Foundational Problems in the Special Sciences 10*(2), 3-33.
8. Wheeler, J. as quoted in Capra, F. (1991). *The Tao of Physics*. Boston, MA: Shambhala Publications.
9. Barrow, J. D., Davies, P. C., & Harper Jr., C. L. (Eds.). (2004). *Science and ultimate reality: Quantum theory, cosmology, and complexity.* Cambridge, UK: Cambridge University Press. (p. 201)
10. Rees, M. (1987). The anthropic universe. *New Scientist, 115*(1572), 44-47.
11. Patton, C. M., & Wheeler, J. A. (1975). Is physics legislated by cosmogony. In C. J. Isham, R. Penrose & D. W. Sciama (Eds.), *Quantum Gravity: Proceedings of the Oxford Symposium* (Vol. 1), (pp. 538-605). Oxford, UK: Clarendon Press. (p. 564.)
12. Linde, A. (2003). Inflation, quantum cosmology and the anthropic principle. In J. D. Barrow, P. C. W. Davies & C. L. Harper Jr (Eds.),

Science and Ultimate Reality: Quantum Theory, Cosmology, and Complexity (426-458). Cambridge, UK: Cambridge University Press.

13. Ibid.
14. Linde, A. (1990). *Particle physics and inflationary cosmology*. New York, NY: Harwood Academic Publishers.
15. Davies, P. (2013). *Paul Davies: Can we explain cosmos and consciousness?* [Video file]. Retrieved from http://www.closertotruth.com
16. Redfern, M. (Presenter) & Deutsch, D. (Speaker). (2006, February 18). [Radio broadcast]. In P. Newman (Producer), The Anthropic Universe, The Science Show. Sydney, Australia: ABC Radio.
17. Redfern, M. (Presenter) & Davies, P. (Speaker). (2006, February 18). [Radio broadcast]. In P. Newman (Producer), The Anthropic Universe, The Science Show. Sydney, Australia: ABC Radio.
18. Speigel, L. (2014, June 24). There are 'tens of billions' of habitable planets in our galaxy, astronomer Seth Shostak says. *Huffington Post*.
19. Kurzweil, R. (2005). *The singularity is near: When humans transcend biology*. New York, NY: Penguin Group.
20. Kurzweil, R. (2013). *Raymond Kurzweil: What is the far future of life in the universe?* [Video file]. Retrieved from: http//:www.closertotruth.com
21. Dyson, F. J. (1971). Energy in the universe. *Scientific American 224*(3), 50-59.
22. De Chardin, P. T. (1999). *The human phenomenon*. (S. Appleton-Weber, Trans.). Sussex, UK: Sussex Academic Press.
23. As quoted in Davies, P. (2006). *The Goldilocks enigma: Why is the universe just right for life?*. London, UK: Penguin Books. (p. 282)

24. Dunne, B. J., & Jahn, R. G. (2005). The PEAR Proposition. *Journal of Scientific Exploration, 19*(2), 195–245.
25. Koch, C. (2013). *Christof Koch: Must the universe contain consciousness?* [Video file]. Retrieved from: http//:www.closertotruth.com
26. Hawking, S. (1988). *A Brief History of Time.* New York, NY: Bantam Dell Publish Group. (p. 174)
27. Chalmers, D. (2014). *David Chalmers: How do you explain consciousness?* [Video file]. Retrieved from http://www.ted.com
28. Sartre, J. P. (2012). *Being and nothingness.* Open Road Media.
29. Hofstadter, D. R. (2008). *I am a strange loop.* Basic books.
30. Blamauer, M. (Ed.). (2011). *The Mental as Fundamental: New Perspectives on Panpsychism.* Walter de Gruyter.
31. Leslie, J. (1979). *Value and existence.* Rowman and Littlefield
32. Davies, P. (2006). *The Goldilocks Enigma: Why is the universe just right for life?.* London, UK: Penguin Books. (p. 294)
33. Searle, J. (2013). *John Searle: Our shared condition – consciousness* [Video file]. Retrieved from www.ted.com
34. Dyson, F. (1988). *Infinite in all directions.* New York, NY: Harper and Row. (p. 297)
35. Nagel, T. (2012). Mind and cosmos: Why the materialist neo-Darwinian conception of nature is almost certainly false. New York, NY: Oxford University Press. (p. 123)
36. Nagel, T. (2012). Mind and cosmos: Why the materialist neo-Darwinian conception of nature is almost certainly false. New York, NY: Oxford University Press. (p. 85)

37. Nagel, T. (2012). *Mind and cosmos: Why the materialist neo-Darwinian conception of nature is almost certainly false.* New York, NY: Oxford University Press. (p. 66)
38. Wright, R. (2000). *Nonzero: The Logic of Human Destiny.* New York, NY: Pantheon Books.
39. Neumann, J., & Morgenstern, O. (1944). *Theory of Games and Economic Behavior,* Princeton, NJ: Princeton University Press.
40. Wright, R. (2000). *Nonzero: The Logic of Human Destiny.* New York, NY: Pantheon Books. (p. 321)
41. Wright, R. (2000). *Nonzero: The Logic of Human Destiny.* New York, NY: Pantheon Books. (p. 135)
42. Wright, R. (2000). *Nonzero: The Logic of Human Destiny.* New York, NY: Pantheon Books. (pp. 316-317)
43. Seligman, M.E.P. (2010). *Authentic Happiness: Using the new positive psychology to realize your potential for lasting fulfilment.* London, UK: Nicholas Brealey Publishing. (p. 256)

Chapter 11. HORIZONS

1. Kant, I., & Pluhar, W. S. (1987). *Critique of judgment.* Hackett Publishing.
2. Nagel, T. (2012). *Mind and cosmos: Why the materialist neo-Darwinian conception of nature is almost certainly false.* New York, NY: Oxford University Press. (p. 3)

3. Koch, C. (2012). *Consciousness: Confessions of a romantic reductionist.* Cambridge, MA: MIT press. (p.132)

4. Paul Davies (1995). Acceptance speech of the Templeton Prize.

5. Radin, D. (2013). *Supernormal: Science, yoga, and the evidence for extraordinary psychic abilities.* New York, NY: Random House, Inc. (p. 6)

6. Capra, F. (1991). *The Tao of Physics.* Boston, MA: Shambhala Publications.

7. Wallace, B. A. (2007). *Hidden dimensions: The unification of physics and consciousness.* Columbia University Press.

8. Dyson, F. (1988). *Infinite in All Directions.* New York, NY: Harper and Row. (p. 297)

9. Tarnas, R. (1991). *The passion of the western mind.* New York, NY: Random House Publishing Ballantine Books. (p. 432)

10. Capra, F. (1996). *The web of life: A new scientific understanding of living systems.* New York, NY: Random House LLC. (p. 4)

11. Skrbina, D. (2005). *Panpsychism in the West.* MA: MIT Press.

12. Skrbina, D. (2005). *Panpsychism in the West.* MA: MIT Press. (p. 265)

13. Skrbina, D. (2005). *Panpsychism in the West.* MA: MIT Press. (p. 268)

14. Keim, B. (2013, November 14). A Neuroscientist's Radical Theory of How Networks Become Conscious. *Wired.*

15. Sheldrake, R. (2012). *Science set free: 10 paths to new discovery.* New York, NY: Random House Inc. (p. 53)

16. Badashi, T. (2015). *Technosophia: A Cosmohumanist Manifesto.* San Francisco.